## Chapter 1: Getting Started

### Introduction: Your First Step Toward Building Business Credit

Welcome to the beginning of an exciting journey toward building strong business credit. Whether you're a new entrepreneur or looking to strengthen your existing business, understanding and managing business credit is crucial to your success. This chapter will guide you through the foundational steps needed to establish your business, laying the groundwork for a robust credit profile that will open doors to growth, financing, and long-term stability.

### Why Business Credit Matters

Before we dive into the technical details, it's important to understand the impact of business credit on your future. Business credit is more than just a score—it's a reflection of your business's financial health and credibility. Here's why building business credit should be a top priority:

1. **Access to Better Financing:**
   - A strong business credit score allows you to secure loans and credit lines at lower interest rates, which can save you thousands of dollars and provide the capital you need to grow.
   - Higher credit limits become available as your credit profile strengthens, offering you more financial flexibility.
2. **Protection of Personal Assets:**

- By building business credit, you can separate your personal and business finances, reducing the risk of your personal assets being affected by business-related debts.
- Personal guarantees, which are often required for new businesses, can be minimized or avoided altogether as your business credit improves.

3. **Establishing Credibility:**
   - A solid credit profile demonstrates to suppliers, lenders, and partners that your business is reliable and financially stable.
   - This credibility can lead to better payment terms, larger trade credit lines, and more favorable business relationships.

4. **Supporting Growth and Expansion:**
   - Strong business credit enables you to take advantage of opportunities that require capital, such as expanding operations, purchasing equipment, or investing in marketing.
   - It positions your business for long-term success, giving you the financial tools to navigate challenges and seize opportunities.

**Understanding the Role of Personal Credit**

At the start, your personal credit will play a significant role in establishing your business credit. Lenders and creditors often look at your personal credit score when assessing the risk of extending credit to a new business. This makes maintaining and improving your personal credit essential in the early stages.

- **Building a Bridge with Personal Credit:**

1. Your personal credit score serves as a bridge until your business establishes its own credit history. A strong personal credit score can help you secure favorable loan terms and credit lines in your business's name.
- **Steps to Improve Personal Credit:**
    1. **Pay Down Existing Debts:** Reducing credit card balances and paying off personal loans lowers your debt-to-income ratio, positively affecting your credit score.
    2. **Correct Errors:** Regularly review your credit report for inaccuracies. Disputing errors with the credit bureaus ensures your credit report accurately reflects your financial behavior.
        - **Resource:** Annual Credit Report - Access your credit report for free.
    3. **Avoid New Inquiries:** Limit new credit applications to avoid hard inquiries, which can temporarily lower your credit score.
        - **Resource:** Credit Karma - A free tool for monitoring and improving your credit score.

These steps are not just about maintaining personal credit but are foundational to setting up your business for financial success.

**Choosing Your Business Structure: LLC vs. S-Corp**

Your choice of business structure significantly impacts your business's legal and financial future. The two most popular structures for small businesses are Limited Liability Companies (LLC) and S Corporations (S-Corp). Here's what you need to know to make an informed decision:

**Limited Liability Company (LLC)**

- **Overview:**
    1. An LLC is a flexible business structure that offers limited liability protection, meaning your personal assets are generally protected from business debts and liabilities. It's a popular choice for small businesses due to its simplicity and tax benefits.
- **Advantages:**
    1. **Limited Liability:** Protects personal assets from business-related risks.
    2. **Tax Flexibility:** Can be taxed as a sole proprietorship, partnership, S-Corp, or C-Corp.
    3. **Ease of Formation:** Less paperwork and formalities compared to a corporation.
    4. **Ownership Flexibility:** No restrictions on the number or type of members.
- **Disadvantages:**
    1. **Self-Employment Taxes:** LLC members may be subject to self-employment taxes on their share of the profits.
    2. **State-Specific Rules:** LLC regulations and fees can vary significantly by state.

## S Corporation (S-Corp)

- **Overview:**
    1. An S-Corp is a corporation that elects to pass corporate income, losses, deductions, and credits through to shareholders for federal tax purposes. This allows for the

avoidance of double taxation—once at the corporate level and again at the individual level.

- **Advantages:**
    1. **Tax Savings:** Shareholders can receive dividends that are not subject to self-employment taxes, potentially reducing tax liability.
    2. **Limited Liability:** Like an LLC, an S-Corp protects personal assets.
    3. **Credibility:** Corporations are often perceived as more credible, which can enhance business relationships.
- **Disadvantages:**
    1. **Stricter Requirements:** Must adhere to IRS requirements, including limits on the number and type of shareholders.
    2. **Increased Formalities:** Requires regular meetings, detailed record-keeping, and adherence to corporate governance rules.

**How to Choose?** Consider the nature of your business, potential for growth, and tax implications when choosing between an LLC and S-Corp. Consult with a tax professional to determine which structure aligns best with your business goals.

**Registering Your Business**

Once you've chosen your business structure, the next step is to register your business. This involves filing the appropriate documents with your state and obtaining necessary identification numbers and permits.

**Paperwork Needed:**

- **Articles of Organization (LLC):** The foundational document for establishing an LLC, outlining the business name, address, and structure.
- **Articles of Incorporation (S-Corp):** Similar to the Articles of Organization but specific to corporations, including details on the corporate structure and stock issuance.
- **Operating Agreement (LLC) and Corporate Bylaws (S-Corp):** Internal documents that govern the management and operation of your business, outlining roles, responsibilities, and decision-making processes.

**How to Register Your Business:**

1. **Choose a Business Name:** Ensure your business name is unique and complies with your state's requirements.
    - **Resource:** USPTO Trademark Search - Check for existing trademarks to avoid conflicts.
2. **File Your Paperwork:** Submit the necessary documents to your state's Secretary of State office. This process can usually be completed online or by mail.
    - **Resource:** Secretary of State Websites - Find your state's filing website.
3. **Obtain an EIN:** An Employer Identification Number (EIN) is required for tax reporting, hiring employees, and opening a business bank account.
    - **Resource:** IRS EIN Application - Apply for your EIN online.
4. **Secure Necessary Licenses and Permits:** Depending on your industry, you may need specific licenses or permits to operate legally.

- **Resource:** SBA Business Licenses & Permits - Guidance on required licenses.

**Opening a Business Bank Account**

Opening a business bank account is a crucial step in separating your personal and business finances. This separation is essential for maintaining legal protection and establishing a clear financial history for your business.

**How to Open an Account:**

1. **Select a Bank:** Choose a bank that offers business accounts with favorable terms and services that meet your needs.
    - **Resource:** NerdWallet's Best Business Bank Accounts - Compare top business bank accounts.
2. **Gather Documents:** You'll need your EIN, Articles of Organization/Incorporation, Operating Agreement/Corporate Bylaws, and a personal ID.
3. **Open the Account:** Visit the bank in person or apply online to open your business checking account. Deposit the required initial funds and set up online banking.

**Why It's Important to Separate Finances:** Separating your personal and business finances is not just about legal protection—it's about creating a financial identity for your business. This separation simplifies accounting, ensures tax compliance, and is crucial for building business credit.

**Free and Low-Cost Resources:**

- **BlueVine Business Banking:** Offers free business checking with no monthly fees, helping you start managing your finances efficiently.
- **Mint:** A free tool for tracking your expenses and managing budgets.

**Encouragement: Laying the Foundation for Success**

Congratulations! By understanding the importance of business credit and taking these initial steps, you've laid a solid foundation for your business's financial success. These early actions—choosing the right structure, registering your business, and separating your finances—are critical in establishing a strong credit profile. Remember, building business credit is a journey, and you're already on the right path. With each step, you're not just building credit—you're building a future for your business filled with opportunities and growth.

## Chapter 2: Separate Finances

In Chapter 1, we laid the groundwork for your business by establishing its legal structure and opening a business bank account. Now, we'll delve deeper into the importance of separating your business finances from your personal ones. This chapter will guide you through setting up the financial systems that will help you manage your business effectively and build a strong credit profile.

## Why Separating Finances is Crucial

One of the most important steps in building and maintaining strong business credit is keeping your personal and business finances separate. Here's why this separation is crucial:

1. **Legal Protection:**
   - **Maintaining Limited Liability:** By separating your finances, you uphold the limited liability protection provided by your LLC or S-Corp. This means that if your business faces financial difficulties or legal issues, your personal assets—such as your home, car, and personal savings—are generally protected.
   - **Avoiding Piercing the Corporate Veil:** Commingling personal and business finances can lead to a legal situation known as "piercing the corporate veil." This can make you personally liable for business debts and obligations. Keeping finances separate ensures that your business remains a distinct legal entity.
2. **Simplified Tax Preparation:**
   - **Clear Financial Records:** Having separate accounts makes it easier to track your business income and expenses, simplifying tax preparation and ensuring that you can take full advantage of business deductions.
   - **Accurate Tax Reporting:** Mixing personal and business finances can lead to errors in tax reporting, potentially resulting

in penalties or audits. Clear separation helps you maintain accurate records and meet tax obligations.
3. **Building Business Credit:**
   - **Establishing a Financial Identity:** A separate business account helps create a financial identity for your business, which is essential for building business credit. Lenders and creditors will look at your business's financial history when assessing creditworthiness.
   - **Easier Credit Monitoring:** With separate finances, it's easier to monitor your business credit activity, ensuring that all payments are made on time and that your credit profile remains strong.
4. **Professionalism:**
   - **Building Trust:** Having a dedicated business bank account and credit card shows that you take your business seriously. It can enhance your credibility with suppliers, clients, and partners, making them more likely to offer favorable terms and trust in your business dealings.

**Getting a Business Credit Card**

A business credit card is a valuable tool for managing expenses, building credit, and separating your business transactions from personal ones. Here's how to choose and use a business credit card effectively:

**Choosing the Right Business Credit Card:**

- **Consider Your Business Needs:**

- Look for a card that offers rewards or cash back in categories where your business spends the most, such as office supplies, travel, or advertising.
- Consider cards with no annual fees or low interest rates if you plan to carry a balance.
- **Check for Reporting:**
  - Ensure the card issuer reports to the business credit bureaus (Dun & Bradstreet, Experian, and Equifax). This reporting is crucial for building your business credit history.
- **Start with a Secured Card If Necessary:**
  - If your business is new or your personal credit isn't strong, consider starting with a secured business credit card. These cards require a cash deposit as collateral but can help you build credit.

**Using Your Business Credit Card Wisely:**

- **Pay On Time:**
  - Timely payments are the single most important factor in building and maintaining strong business credit. Set up automatic payments or reminders to ensure you never miss a due date.
- **Keep Utilization Low:**
  - Aim to use no more than 30% of your credit limit. High utilization can negatively impact your credit score, even if you pay off the balance each month.
- **Monitor Your Statements:**

- Regularly review your credit card statements to ensure all charges are accurate and to track your spending. This helps you spot any unauthorized transactions and stay within your budget.
- **Separate Personal and Business Expenses:**
  - Use your business credit card exclusively for business-related purchases. This not only helps with bookkeeping but also strengthens the separation between personal and business finances.

**Free and Low-Cost Resources:**

- **Credit Karma:** A free service that offers credit monitoring and advice for improving both personal and business credit.
- **Nav.com:** Provides business credit reports and tools for building credit, with free and paid options.

**Opening a Business Savings Account**

In addition to a checking account, consider opening a business savings account. This can help you set aside funds for taxes, future investments, or emergency expenses. A business savings account also allows you to earn interest on your reserves, contributing to your business's financial health.

**Benefits of a Business Savings Account:**

- **Tax Savings:** Set aside a portion of your income in a savings account to cover quarterly tax payments. This helps you avoid last-minute scrambles for cash when taxes are due.

- **Emergency Fund:** Building a reserve in a savings account provides a financial cushion in case of unexpected expenses or a downturn in business.
- **Earning Interest:** Many business savings accounts offer interest on your balance, helping your money grow over time.

**Managing Cash Flow**

Effective cash flow management is essential for keeping your business running smoothly and ensuring that you can meet your financial obligations. Here are some tips for managing cash flow:

**Forecasting and Budgeting:**

- **Create a Cash Flow Forecast:** Estimate your business's income and expenses for the next month, quarter, or year. This helps you anticipate any shortfalls and plan accordingly.
- **Stick to a Budget:** Create a budget based on your forecast and track your actual income and expenses against it. Adjust as necessary to stay within your means.

**Invoicing and Payment Terms:**

- **Invoice Promptly:** Send invoices as soon as work is completed or goods are delivered. The sooner you invoice, the sooner you'll get paid.
- **Set Clear Payment Terms:** Establish clear payment terms with your clients, such as net-30 or net-60, and follow up promptly on overdue invoices.

**Managing Receivables:**

- **Offer Early Payment Discounts:** Encourage clients to pay early by offering a small discount for payments made within a specified period.
- **Implement a Collections Process:** Have a plan in place for following up on late payments. This may include sending reminder emails, making phone calls, or working with a collections agency.

**Free and Low-Cost Resources:**

- **Wave:** A free accounting software that includes invoicing and payment tracking, helping you manage cash flow effectively.
- **QuickBooks:** An accounting software that offers more advanced features for managing cash flow, budgeting, and forecasting.

**Encouragement: Strengthening Your Financial Foundation**

By separating your finances, managing cash flow, and using a business credit card responsibly, you're laying the foundation for a financially stable and successful business. These practices not only protect your personal assets but also position your business to build strong credit, secure better financing, and grow confidently. Remember, the habits you establish now will shape your business's financial future. Stay disciplined, keep learning, and continue to strengthen your financial foundation.

## Chapter 3: Establishing Vendor Credit

Establishing vendor credit is one of the most straightforward ways to build your business credit profile. Vendor credit, also known as trade credit, involves purchasing goods or services from suppliers on credit and paying for them later—typically within 30, 60, or 90 days. This chapter will guide you through choosing the right vendors, managing your trade credit effectively, and leveraging these relationships to build a strong credit history.

### Why Vendor Credit is Important

Vendor credit is a foundational element of your business's credit profile. Here's why it's so crucial:

1. **Building Credit History:**
   - **Reporting to Bureaus:** Many vendors report your payment history to business credit bureaus like Dun & Bradstreet, Experian, and Equifax. Timely payments can help establish a positive credit history for your business.
   - **Starting Small:** Even if you're a new business with no credit history, vendors are often willing to extend small lines of credit, which you can gradually increase over time.
2. **Improving Cash Flow:**
   - **Delayed Payments:** Vendor credit allows you to receive goods or services immediately and pay for them later, giving you more flexibility in managing your cash flow.

- **No Interest Charges:** Unlike loans or credit cards, vendor credit often comes with no interest, as long as you pay within the agreed-upon terms.
3. **Building Relationships:**
    - **Strengthening Business Ties:** Establishing good relationships with vendors can lead to better terms, discounts, and priority service. Vendors may also be more flexible in times of financial difficulty if you have a strong payment history with them.
4. **Enhancing Credibility:**
    - **Demonstrating Reliability:** Consistent, on-time payments to vendors demonstrate your business's reliability and financial stability. This can enhance your credibility with other lenders, suppliers, and business partners.

**Choosing the Right Vendors**

Selecting the right vendors is crucial for building your business credit. Here's how to identify and choose vendors that can help you establish and grow your credit profile:

**Criteria for Choosing Vendors:**

- **Reports to Credit Bureaus:** Ensure that the vendor reports payment history to one or more business credit bureaus. This is essential for building your credit profile.
- **Terms That Match Your Cash Flow:** Look for vendors that offer payment terms (e.g., net-30, net-60) that align with your business's cash flow needs. This gives you enough time to generate revenue from the goods or services before the payment is due.

- **Industry Relevance:** Choose vendors that provide goods or services relevant to your business. This ensures that the credit you're establishing is not only beneficial for building credit but also supports your business operations.
- **Willingness to Work with New Businesses:** If you're just starting out, look for vendors that are known for working with new businesses and extending credit even if you have little or no business credit history.

**How to Approach Vendors:**

1. **Start Small:** Begin by placing small orders with a few vendors. This helps you establish a payment history without overextending your finances.
2. **Pay Early:** Whenever possible, pay your invoices early. This not only builds a positive payment history but can also lead to better terms with the vendor in the future.
3. **Communicate:** Keep open lines of communication with your vendors. If you ever foresee a delay in payment, inform the vendor in advance and work out a solution. This shows professionalism and can help maintain a good relationship.

**List of 25 Vendors that Report to Business Credit Bureaus**

Here is a curated list of 25 vendors that report to business credit bureaus. These vendors offer credit terms that can help you establish and build your business credit:

1. **Uline**

- Industry: Shipping, Packaging, and Industrial Supplies
- Credit Terms: Net-30
- Reports to: Dun & Bradstreet, Experian
- Website: Uline
2. Grainger
    - Industry: Industrial Supplies and Equipment
    - Credit Terms: Net-30
    - Reports to: Dun & Bradstreet, Experian
    - Website: Grainger
3. Quill
    - Industry: Office Supplies and Furniture
    - Credit Terms: Net-30
    - Reports to: Dun & Bradstreet
    - Website: Quill
4. Summa Office Supplies
    - Industry: Office Supplies
    - Credit Terms: Net-30
    - Reports to: Dun & Bradstreet, Experian, Equifax
    - Website: Summa Office Supplies
5. Crown Office Supplies
    - Industry: Office Supplies
    - Credit Terms: Net-30
    - Reports to: Dun & Bradstreet, Equifax, Experian
    - Website: Crown Office Supplies
6. Strategic Network Solutions
    - Industry: IT and Networking Solutions
    - Credit Terms: Net-30

- Reports to: Equifax, CreditSafe
- Website: Strategic Network Solutions
7. **Shirtsy**
    - **Industry:** Custom Apparel and Printing
    - **Credit Terms:** Net-30
    - **Reports to:** Equifax, CreditSafe, Ansonia
    - **Website:** Shirtsy
8. **Wise Business Plans**
    - **Industry:** Business Plan Writing Services
    - **Credit Terms:** Net-30
    - **Reports to:** Equifax, Experian
    - **Website:** Wise Business Plans
9. **Office Garner**
    - **Industry:** Office Supplies
    - **Credit Terms:** Net-30
    - **Reports to:** Equifax, Experian
    - **Website:** Office Garner
10. **Business T-Shirt Club**
    - **Industry:** Custom Apparel and Promotional Items
    - **Credit Terms:** Net-30
    - **Reports to:** Equifax
    - **Website:** Business T-Shirt Club
11. **Nav**
    - **Industry:** Business Credit Monitoring
    - **Credit Terms:** Net-30 (for premium services)
    - **Reports to:** Experian, Dun & Bradstreet, Equifax
    - **Website:** Nav

12. **Creative Analytics**
    - **Industry:** Digital Marketing and Analytics
    - **Credit Terms:** Net-30
    - **Reports to:** Equifax
    - **Website:** Creative Analytics
13. **Ohana Office Products**
    - **Industry:** Office Supplies
    - **Credit Terms:** Net-30
    - **Reports to:** Equifax
    - **Website:** Ohana Office Products
14. **The CEO Creative**
    - **Industry:** Marketing and Creative Services
    - **Credit Terms:** Net-30
    - **Reports to:** Equifax, CreditSafe
    - **Website:** The CEO Creative
15. **Seton**
    - **Industry:** Safety, Labels, and Compliance Products
    - **Credit Terms:** Net-30
    - **Reports to:** Dun & Bradstreet
    - **Website:** Seton
16. **Monopolize Your Marketplace**
    - **Industry:** Marketing and Advertising Services
    - **Credit Terms:** Net-30
    - **Reports to:** Equifax
    - **Website:** Monopolize Your Marketplace
17. **Kabbage**
    - **Industry:** Small Business Loans and Credit Lines

- Credit Terms: Revolving Credit Lines
- Reports to: Experian, Equifax, Dun & Bradstreet
- Website: Kabbage

18. **CJF Global**
    - **Industry:** Office Supplies and Services
    - **Credit Terms:** Net-30
    - **Reports to:** Equifax, Experian
    - **Website:** CJF Global

19. **eCredable**
    - **Industry:** Utility and Telecom Payment Reporting
    - **Credit Terms:** N/A (reports utility and telecom payments)
    - **Reports to:** Equifax, Experian
    - **Website:** eCredable

20. **4imprint**
    - **Industry:** Promotional Products
    - **Credit Terms:** Net-30
    - **Reports to:** Dun & Bradstreet
    - **Website:** 4imprint

21. **Gempler's**
    - **Industry:** Outdoor Workwear and Supplies
    - **Credit Terms:** Net-30
    - **Reports to:** Dun & Bradstreet
    - **Website:** Gempler's

22. **Marlin Business Services**
    - **Industry:** Business Equipment Financing
    - **Credit Terms:** Equipment Lease Financing
    - **Reports to:** Experian, Dun & Bradstreet, Equifax

- Website: Marlin Business Services
23. **Capital One Trade Credit (formerly BlueTarp)**
    - **Industry:** B2B Financing Solutions
    - **Credit Terms:** Net-30 or Revolving Credit
    - **Reports to:** Experian, Equifax
    - **Website:** Capital One Trade Credit
24. **MSC Industrial Supply**
    - **Industry:** Industrial Supplies
    - **Credit Terms:** Net-30
    - **Reports to:** Dun & Bradstreet, Experian
    - **Website:** MSC Industrial Supply
25. **Fastenal**
    - **Industry:** Industrial and Construction Supplies
    - **Credit Terms:** Net-30
    - **Reports to:** Dun & Bradstreet, Experian
    - **Website:** Fastenal

**How to Use These Vendors to Build Credit**

Once you've selected your vendors, it's important to manage your relationships and credit lines effectively. Here's how to use these vendors to build strong business credit:

1. **Start Small:**
    - Begin by placing small orders to establish your creditworthiness. This helps build trust with the vendor and ensures you can manage your payments comfortably.
2. **Pay Early:**

- Whenever possible, pay your invoices before the due date. Early payments can enhance your reputation with vendors and may even lead to more favorable terms in the future.
3. **Monitor Your Credit:**
    - Regularly check your business credit reports to ensure that your payments are being reported accurately by the vendors. This helps you spot any discrepancies and maintain a positive credit profile.
    - **Resource:** Nav.com - A tool for monitoring your business credit.
4. **Expand Gradually:**
    - As your relationship with the vendors strengthens, gradually increase your order sizes. This not only helps you build credit but also allows you to take advantage of better terms and discounts.

**Free and Low-Cost Resources**

Building vendor credit doesn't have to be expensive. Here are some free and low-cost resources to help you along the way:

- **Nav:** Offers free tools to monitor your business credit and advice on how to improve it.
- **CreditSafe:** Provides business credit reports and monitoring services at competitive prices.
- **Credit Builder Services:** Some companies offer credit-building services that work directly with vendors to help you establish and grow your business credit.

**Encouragement: Laying the Building Blocks of Success**

Establishing vendor credit is like laying the building blocks of your business's financial foundation. Each on-time payment adds to your credit history, strengthening your business's reputation and financial health. Remember, building business credit is a marathon, not a sprint. Start small, stay consistent, and watch as your credit profile grows, opening doors to better financing, more opportunities, and a thriving business future.

## Chapter 4: Paying Bills On Time

In the previous chapter, we discussed how establishing vendor credit is a crucial step in building your business credit profile. Now, we'll focus on one of the most important aspects of maintaining and improving that credit: paying your bills on time. Timely payments are not just a good business practice—they are the cornerstone of a strong credit profile. This chapter will guide you through the strategies and tools you can use to ensure that your business consistently meets its financial obligations.

**Why Paying Bills On Time is Crucial**

Timely payments are the most significant factor in determining your business credit score. Here's why it's so crucial:

1. **Direct Impact on Credit Score:**
   - **Payment History:** Payment history is the most heavily weighted factor in business credit scoring models. Consistently paying bills on time or early can significantly boost your credit score.
   - **Late Payments:** Even one late payment can harm your credit score, making it harder to secure financing or negotiate favorable terms with suppliers in the future.
2. **Building Trust with Creditors:**
   - **Establishing Reliability:** When you pay your bills on time, you build trust with your creditors. This can lead to better terms, such as higher credit limits, lower interest rates, and extended payment terms.
   - **Strengthening Relationships:** Strong relationships with vendors, lenders, and creditors can be vital in times of financial difficulty. If you've built a history of timely payments, creditors may be more willing to work with you if you need flexibility.
3. **Avoiding Penalties and Fees:**
   - **Late Fees:** Late payments often result in penalties, which can add unnecessary costs to your business. These fees can be avoided by staying on top of your payment schedule.
   - **Interest Charges:** Some creditors may charge interest on overdue balances, increasing your costs and potentially leading to a cycle of debt that's difficult to escape.
4. **Supporting Cash Flow Management:**
   - **Predictable Cash Flow:** Paying bills on time helps you maintain predictable cash flow, which is essential for managing

day-to-day operations, planning for future expenses, and making informed financial decisions.

**Setting Up Automatic Payments**

One of the most effective ways to ensure that your bills are paid on time is to set up automatic payments. This strategy removes the risk of forgetting due dates and helps you stay consistent with your payments.

**Benefits of Automatic Payments:**

- **Consistency:** Automatic payments ensure that your bills are paid on time, every time, without requiring constant attention.
- **Time Savings:** Automating your payments frees up time that can be better spent on other aspects of running your business.
- **Avoiding Human Error:** By automating payments, you eliminate the risk of missed payments due to oversight or human error.

**How to Set Up Automatic Payments:**

1. **Identify Recurring Bills:**
   - Make a list of bills that are due on a regular basis, such as utilities, rent, vendor payments, and loan installments.
2. **Check for Automatic Payment Options:**
   - Contact your vendors, service providers, and lenders to see if they offer automatic payment options. Most do, and many allow you to set up payments directly through their websites or customer service portals.
3. **Use Online Banking:**

- Most banks offer online bill pay services that allow you to schedule recurring payments. This is particularly useful if a vendor or service provider does not offer their own automatic payment option.
4. **Monitor Your Accounts:**
    - Even with automatic payments set up, it's important to regularly monitor your accounts to ensure that payments are being processed correctly and that there are sufficient funds in your account to cover each payment.

**Cautions When Using Automatic Payments:**

- **Ensure Sufficient Funds:** Always make sure you have enough funds in your account to cover automatic payments. Overdraft fees can add up quickly if you're not careful.
- **Review Statements Regularly:** Regularly review your bank and credit card statements to ensure all payments are accurate and no unauthorized transactions have occurred.

**Handling Cash Flow Issues**

Even with the best planning, businesses can sometimes face cash flow challenges that make it difficult to pay bills on time. Here's how to handle these situations effectively:

**Prioritizing Payments:**

- **Critical Bills First:** Prioritize paying bills that are critical to keeping your business operational, such as rent, utilities, and payroll. These are essential for maintaining day-to-day operations.

- **Bills That Affect Credit:** Pay bills that report to credit bureaus next. These payments directly impact your business credit score, so they should be a high priority.
- **Negotiate Payment Terms:** If you anticipate cash flow issues, contact your creditors before the payment is due to negotiate extended payment terms. Many creditors are willing to work with you if you have a history of timely payments.

**Short-Term Financing Options:**

- **Business Line of Credit:** If you're facing temporary cash flow issues, consider using a business line of credit. This can provide the necessary funds to cover expenses without disrupting your payment schedule.
- **Invoice Financing:** If your business relies on invoicing clients, consider invoice financing. This allows you to borrow against your accounts receivable, providing immediate cash flow while you wait for clients to pay.
    - **Resource:** Fundbox - Provides quick, flexible loans and invoice financing for small businesses.

**Monitoring and Adjusting Cash Flow:**

- **Cash Flow Forecasting:** Regularly update your cash flow forecast to anticipate future shortfalls and plan accordingly. This can help you make informed decisions about when to seek additional financing or when to cut back on expenses.

- **Expense Management:** Review your business expenses regularly to identify areas where you can cut costs or delay non-essential purchases. This can free up cash to cover more critical expenses.

**Dealing with Late Payments**

If you've missed a payment, it's important to address the situation promptly to minimize the impact on your credit score and business relationships.

**Steps to Take After Missing a Payment:**

1. **Contact the Creditor Immediately:**
   - Reach out to the creditor as soon as you realize a payment is late. Explain the situation and ask if they can waive any late fees or penalties. Many creditors are willing to accommodate one-time lapses if you've been a reliable payer in the past.
2. **Make the Payment as Soon as Possible:**
   - Pay the overdue bill as quickly as you can to minimize the impact on your credit score. The longer a payment is overdue, the more it can hurt your credit.
3. **Monitor Your Credit Report:**
   - Keep an eye on your credit report to see how the late payment is affecting your score. If the payment was late due to an error (such as a bank processing delay), dispute the negative mark with the credit bureau.
4. **Prevent Future Late Payments:**
   - Review what led to the missed payment and take steps to prevent it from happening again. This might involve setting up

automatic payments, adjusting your cash flow management, or creating reminders for upcoming due dates.

**Free and Low-Cost Resources**

There are several tools and resources available to help you manage payments and avoid late fees:

- **Mint:** A free financial management tool that helps you track your income, expenses, and upcoming bills. It also allows you to set up alerts for payment due dates.
- **QuickBooks:** While not free, QuickBooks offers robust accounting software that includes features for tracking bills, setting up automatic payments, and managing cash flow. It's a worthwhile investment for businesses that need more advanced financial management tools.
- **Wave:** A free accounting software that includes invoicing and bill management, making it easier to keep track of payments and due dates.

**Encouragement: Staying Consistent and Building Momentum**

Paying your bills on time is about more than just avoiding penalties—it's about building a solid foundation for your business's financial health. Each on-time payment strengthens your credit profile, builds trust with creditors, and helps you manage your business with confidence. While managing cash flow and ensuring timely payments can be challenging, especially for new businesses, staying consistent in your efforts will pay off in the long run. Remember, each payment you make on time is a step closer to stronger business credit, better financing options, and long-term success.

## Chapter 5: Monitoring Your Credit

In the previous chapters, we've covered the essential steps to start building your business credit, from setting up your business structure to establishing vendor credit and paying your bills on time. Now, it's time to focus on monitoring your business credit. Regularly monitoring your credit allows you to stay informed about your credit profile, catch errors early, and ensure that all your hard work is reflected in your credit score. This chapter will guide you through the importance of credit monitoring, how to do it effectively, and how to handle disputes if errors are found.

### Why Monitoring Your Business Credit Matters

1. **Staying Informed:**
    - **Real-Time Updates:** Regular credit monitoring keeps you updated on your business's financial health. You'll receive alerts about changes to your credit score, new accounts opened in your name, or any significant shifts in your credit profile.
    - **Proactive Management:** By staying informed, you can make proactive decisions about your finances, such as adjusting spending or addressing any potential issues before they become significant problems.

2. **Detecting Errors Early:**
   - **Common Errors:** Errors on your credit report can include incorrect payment information, accounts that don't belong to you, or outdated information. These errors can negatively impact your credit score if not addressed promptly.
   - **Immediate Action:** Monitoring your credit allows you to catch these errors quickly and take immediate action to dispute them, minimizing any potential damage to your credit score.
3. **Protecting Against Fraud:**
   - **Fraud Alerts:** Regular credit monitoring helps you detect fraudulent activity, such as identity theft or unauthorized accounts opened in your business's name. Early detection is crucial for preventing further damage and resolving the issue swiftly.
   - **Maintaining Trust:** Protecting your business from fraud not only safeguards your financial health but also maintains the trust of your customers, vendors, and partners.
4. **Planning for the Future:**
   - **Setting Goals:** Monitoring your credit helps you set realistic financial goals for your business. You can track your progress over time and see how your efforts to build credit are paying off.
   - **Preparing for Financing:** If you're planning to apply for a loan or line of credit, regular credit monitoring ensures you're fully aware of your credit standing, allowing you to make informed decisions and secure the best possible terms.

**How to Monitor Your Business Credit**

There are several methods and tools available to help you monitor your business credit effectively:

**1. Sign Up for Credit Monitoring Services:**

- **Credit Monitoring Services:** Various companies offer credit monitoring services that provide real-time alerts, access to your business credit reports, and credit score tracking. These services can be free or paid, depending on the features you need.
- **Recommended Services:**
    - **Nav:** Nav offers both free and paid plans for monitoring your business credit. It provides access to your credit reports from multiple bureaus, real-time alerts, and insights into how to improve your credit score.
    - **Dun & Bradstreet CreditSignal:** This free service alerts you to changes in your D&B credit file, helping you stay informed about your PAYDEX score and other key metrics.
    - **Experian Business Credit Advantage:** A paid service that offers daily monitoring of your Experian business credit report, including alerts for changes and access to detailed credit data.

**2. Review Your Credit Reports Regularly:**

- **Accessing Your Reports:** Even if you don't use a credit monitoring service, you should regularly review your business credit reports from the major bureaus: Dun & Bradstreet, Experian, and Equifax. This ensures that all information is accurate and up to date.
- **What to Look For:** When reviewing your reports, check for accurate payment history, correct account information, and any new accounts

that you didn't open. Make sure your business's legal name, address, and other identifying information are correct.

3. **Use Free Tools for Monitoring:**

- **Credit Monitoring Apps:** Some apps, like Credit Karma or NerdWallet, offer free credit monitoring tools that can help you track your business credit score and get alerts for any significant changes. These tools are more commonly used for personal credit but can still be valuable for small business owners.
- **Banking Services:** Some business bank accounts or credit cards offer free credit monitoring as part of their service package. Check with your bank to see if this is available to you.

**Disputing Errors on Your Credit Report**

If you find errors on your business credit report, it's important to address them immediately to prevent any negative impact on your credit score. Here's how to dispute errors effectively:

1. **Gather Documentation:**

- **Proof of Payment:** If the error involves an incorrect payment history, gather bank statements, payment confirmations, and invoices that prove your payment was made on time.
- **Business Records:** For errors related to your business's identity, such as incorrect addresses or ownership information, provide official business documents that show the correct details.

2. **Contact the Credit Bureau:**

- **Submit a Dispute:** Each credit bureau has a process for disputing errors on your credit report. You can usually submit a dispute online, by mail, or by phone. Include all relevant documentation to support your claim.
- **Credit Bureau Contacts:**
    - **Dun & Bradstreet:** Visit the D&B website to submit a dispute online or contact their customer service for assistance.
    - **Experian:** Use the Experian website to file a dispute, providing the necessary documentation.
    - **Equifax:** Equifax offers an online dispute resolution center where you can submit disputes and track their progress.

3. Follow Up:

- **Check for Resolution:** After submitting your dispute, follow up with the credit bureau to ensure the error is corrected. This can take time, so be patient but persistent.
- **Monitor for Changes:** Once the dispute is resolved, check your credit report to confirm that the correction has been made and that your credit score reflects the updated information.

4. Keep Records:

- **Document Everything:** Keep detailed records of all communications with the credit bureaus, including copies of your dispute, any correspondence, and the final resolution. This documentation is important if you need to escalate the issue or refer back to it in the future.

**Using Credit Monitoring to Improve Your Credit**

Monitoring your business credit isn't just about detecting errors—it's also a powerful tool for improving your credit score over time. Here's how you can use credit monitoring to enhance your business's financial health:

**1. Set Credit Goals:**

- **Target Your Score:** Set specific goals for improving your business credit score. For example, you might aim to increase your score by a certain number of points within the next six months.
- **Track Progress:** Use your credit monitoring tools to track your progress toward these goals. Seeing incremental improvements can be motivating and help you stay focused on your financial objectives.

**2. Identify Weaknesses:**

- **Analyze Your Report:** Look for areas where your credit score may be lacking, such as high credit utilization, late payments, or a limited credit history. Understanding these weaknesses allows you to address them directly.
- **Take Action:** For example, if your credit utilization is high, work on paying down balances. If your history is limited, consider opening new trade lines or vendor accounts.

**3. Leverage Positive Activity:**

- **Build on Success:** If your monitoring reveals positive activity—such as on-time payments or low credit utilization—make sure to continue

these practices. Consistency is key to maintaining and improving your credit score.
- **Communicate with Creditors:** If you've built a strong credit history with certain vendors or creditors, ask if they can increase your credit limit or offer better terms. This not only benefits your cash flow but can also positively impact your credit score.

**Free and Low-Cost Resources**

There are several affordable resources available to help you monitor and manage your business credit:

- **Nav:** Provides a range of free and paid tools for monitoring your business credit, along with personalized advice on how to improve your score.
- **Dun & Bradstreet CreditSignal:** A free service that alerts you to changes in your D&B credit file, helping you stay informed and proactive.
- **Experian Business Credit Reports:** Offers low-cost access to your business credit report, along with monitoring services and credit-building tools.

**Encouragement: Taking Control of Your Financial Future**

Monitoring your business credit is more than just a precaution—it's an empowering practice that gives you control over your business's financial future. By staying informed, catching errors early, and using your credit monitoring tools to guide your decisions, you can ensure that your business credit profile remains strong and continues to grow. Remember, your business credit score is a reflection of your hard work, financial responsibility, and dedication to success. Keep a close eye on it, and you'll be well-positioned to achieve your financial goals.

## Chapter 6: Applying for Business Loans

As you've been building your business credit, you may now be in a position to leverage that credit to secure financing. Business loans can provide the capital needed for growth, expansion, or managing cash flow. However, the process of applying for a business loan can be daunting, especially for new entrepreneurs. This chapter will guide you through the steps of applying for a business loan, understanding different types of loans, and ensuring you secure the best possible terms.

**Why Business Loans Are Important**

1. **Fueling Growth:**
   - **Expansion:** Whether you're opening a new location, hiring more staff, or investing in new equipment, a business loan can provide the necessary capital to grow your business.
   - **Marketing and Development:** Loans can also fund marketing campaigns or product development, helping you reach new customers and increase revenue.
2. **Managing Cash Flow:**

- Seasonal Fluctuations: For businesses that experience seasonal sales, loans can help smooth out cash flow during slower periods, ensuring you can meet your financial obligations.
- Unexpected Expenses: Loans can also provide a safety net for unexpected expenses, such as emergency repairs or sudden increases in demand.

3. Building Credit:
   - Establishing a History: Successfully managing a business loan by making timely payments can strengthen your credit profile, making it easier to secure larger loans or better terms in the future.

**Types of Business Loans**

There are several types of business loans available, each suited to different needs. Understanding these options can help you choose the right one for your business:

**1. Term Loans:**

- **Overview:** A term loan provides a lump sum of capital that you repay over a fixed period, usually with a fixed interest rate. These loans are typically used for significant investments, such as purchasing equipment or expanding operations.
- **Pros:** Predictable payments, longer repayment terms, can fund large projects.
- **Cons:** May require collateral, stricter qualification criteria.

**2. Business Lines of Credit:**
- **Overview:** A business line of credit provides access to a set amount of funds that you can draw from as needed. You only pay interest on the amount you use, and once repaid, the credit is available again.
- **Pros:** Flexibility in borrowing, interest-only on drawn amounts, good for managing cash flow.
- **Cons:** May have variable interest rates, annual fees.

**3. SBA Loans:**
- **Overview:** SBA (Small Business Administration) loans are government-backed loans that offer favorable terms and lower interest rates. They are available through participating lenders and are often used for long-term financing.
- **Pros:** Lower interest rates, longer repayment terms, government-backed.
- **Cons:** Lengthy application process, stringent requirements.

**4. Equipment Financing:**
- **Overview:** This type of loan is specifically used to purchase equipment, which serves as collateral. It's a good option for businesses needing machinery, vehicles, or technology.
- **Pros:** Easier approval, equipment acts as collateral, preserves cash flow.
- **Cons:** Limited to equipment purchases, may require a down payment.

**5. Invoice Financing:**

- **Overview:** Invoice financing allows you to borrow against your outstanding invoices. It provides immediate cash flow while you wait for clients to pay.
- **Pros:** Quick access to cash, no need for collateral, based on accounts receivable.
- **Cons:** Can be expensive, fees based on invoice value.

6. Microloans:

- **Overview:** Microloans are small loans typically offered by non-profit organizations or community lenders. They are designed to help small businesses or startups with limited access to traditional financing.
- **Pros:** Easier to qualify for, smaller loan amounts, supportive of new businesses.
- **Cons:** Smaller loan amounts, higher interest rates in some cases.

**How to Prepare for a Business Loan Application**

Before applying for a loan, it's crucial to prepare thoroughly to increase your chances of approval and secure the best terms:

**1. Review Your Business Credit:**

- **Check Your Credit Reports:** Ensure your business credit reports are accurate and up to date. Address any errors or discrepancies before applying.
- **Know Your Score:** Understand your business credit score and how it may impact your loan terms. A higher score can help you secure better interest rates and terms.

**2. Gather Necessary Documentation:**

- **Business Plan:** Many lenders will require a detailed business plan that outlines your business's goals, financial projections, and how you plan to use the loan.
- **Financial Statements:** Prepare your income statements, balance sheets, and cash flow statements. These documents provide insight into your business's financial health.
- **Tax Returns:** Have at least two years of business and personal tax returns ready to demonstrate your income and financial stability.
- **Legal Documents:** Depending on the lender, you may need to provide your business's legal structure documents, such as Articles of Incorporation, operating agreements, or licenses.

**3. Understand Loan Terms:**

- **Interest Rates:** Compare interest rates across different lenders and loan products. Understand whether the rate is fixed or variable and how it will affect your monthly payments.
- **Repayment Terms:** Consider the length of the loan term and how it aligns with your business's cash flow. Longer terms mean lower monthly payments but more interest paid over time.
- **Fees:** Be aware of any fees associated with the loan, such as origination fees, prepayment penalties, or late payment fees.

**4. Determine the Loan Amount:**

- **Assess Your Needs:** Calculate the exact amount of capital you need and avoid borrowing more than necessary. Borrowing too much can

lead to higher debt and interest payments, while borrowing too little can leave you underfunded.
- **Consider Your Ability to Repay:** Ensure that your business can handle the monthly payments without straining your cash flow.

### 5. Choose the Right Lender:

- **Traditional Banks:** Offer a variety of loan products but may have stricter requirements and a longer approval process.
- **Online Lenders:** Provide faster approval and more flexible terms but may charge higher interest rates.
- **Community Lenders:** Often more willing to work with small businesses or startups, offering personalized service and support.

## The Loan Application Process

Here's a step-by-step guide to applying for a business loan:

### 1. Complete the Loan Application:

- **Fill Out the Form:** Whether applying online or in person, complete the loan application with accurate and detailed information.
- **Attach Documentation:** Submit all required documents, including your business plan, financial statements, tax returns, and legal documents.
- **Provide Collateral Information:** If the loan requires collateral, be prepared to provide details about the assets you're offering as security.

### 2. Underwriting and Approval:

- **Lender Review:** The lender will review your application, assess your creditworthiness, and determine the risk of lending to your business.
- **Credit Check:** Expect the lender to perform a credit check on both your business and personal credit profiles.
- **Approval Decision:** The lender will either approve or deny your loan application based on their assessment. If approved, they will present you with the loan terms.

3. Review and Accept the Loan Terms:

- **Carefully Review Terms:** Before accepting the loan, review the terms carefully. Ensure you understand the interest rate, repayment schedule, fees, and any other conditions.
- **Negotiate if Necessary:** If there are terms you're not satisfied with, don't hesitate to negotiate with the lender. You may be able to secure a better deal by discussing your needs and offering additional collateral or guarantees.

4. Sign the Loan Agreement:

- **Formalize the Agreement:** Once you're satisfied with the terms, sign the loan agreement. This legally binds you to the loan's terms and conditions.
- **Receive Funds:** After signing, the lender will disburse the loan funds to your business bank account.

5. Repay the Loan:

- **Make Timely Payments:** Ensure that you make all loan payments on time to avoid penalties and protect your credit score.

- **Automate Payments:** Consider setting up automatic payments to avoid missing due dates.

## Tips for Successfully Managing a Business Loan

Successfully managing a business loan involves more than just making payments on time. Here are some tips to help you get the most out of your financing:

### 1. Use the Loan Wisely:

- **Stick to the Plan:** Use the loan funds strictly for the purposes outlined in your business plan. Avoid using the loan for non-essential expenses that don't contribute to your business's growth or stability.
- **Track Spending:** Keep detailed records of how the loan funds are used. This not only helps you stay on budget but also provides documentation if the lender requires it.

### 2. Monitor Your Financial Health:

- **Review Financial Statements:** Regularly review your financial statements to ensure that your business is on track to meet its financial goals and that you're able to handle the loan repayments.
- **Adjust as Needed:** If your financial situation changes, be proactive in adjusting your budget or loan repayment strategy. This might involve cutting costs, increasing revenue, or refinancing the loan.

### 3. Communicate with Your Lender:

- **Stay in Touch:** Maintain open communication with your lender, especially if you foresee any difficulties in making payments. Many lenders are willing to work with you to find solutions, such as modifying payment schedules or extending the loan term.

**4. Plan for Future Financing:**

- **Build Your Credit:** Successfully managing your current loan will improve your credit profile, making it easier to secure future financing with better terms.
- **Set New Goals:** As your business grows, continue setting financial goals that align with your long-term vision. Whether it's expanding to new markets or investing in new technology, strategic use of financing can help you achieve these goals.

**Free and Low-Cost Resources**

There are several resources available to help you navigate the business loan application process:

- **SBA Loan Resources:** The Small Business Administration offers a wealth of information on their loan programs, including guides on how to apply and what to expect during the process.
- **Nav:** Nav provides a range of tools to help you find the best financing options based on your business credit profile, with personalized recommendations and tips.
- **Lender Match (SBA):** A free tool that connects small businesses with SBA-approved lenders.

**Encouragement: Empowering Your Business with the Right Financing**

Applying for a business loan is a significant step in your business journey, and it can provide the financial boost needed to achieve your goals. By understanding your options, preparing thoroughly, and managing the loan responsibly, you're not just borrowing money—you're investing in the future of your business. Remember, each payment you make on time, each goal you achieve with the help of the loan, is a testament to your business's strength and potential. Keep your eyes on your objectives, and let the right financing empower your path to success.

## Chapter 7: Good Financial Habits

Establishing and maintaining good financial habits is key to the long-term success of your business and the strength of your business credit. While getting credit and loans is essential, how you manage your finances on a day-to-day basis plays a significant role in your business's overall financial health. This chapter will guide you through essential financial habits that will help you keep your business credit strong, maintain cash flow, and set your business up for sustainable growth.

**Why Good Financial Habits Matter**

1. **Consistency is Key:**
    - **Building a Strong Credit Profile:** Consistent financial management ensures that your business remains creditworthy

over time. Lenders and creditors look for businesses that demonstrate reliability and stability.
    - **Long-Term Success:** Good financial habits contribute to the long-term success of your business by promoting financial discipline, ensuring that you can meet obligations, and positioning you to take advantage of growth opportunities.
2. **Avoiding Financial Pitfalls:**
    - **Preventing Debt Accumulation:** By managing your finances carefully, you can avoid unnecessary debt accumulation and the high costs associated with interest and fees.
    - **Minimizing Risks:** Sound financial practices help you anticipate and manage risks, from unexpected expenses to economic downturns.
3. **Improving Cash Flow:**
    - **Smoother Operations:** Effective cash flow management allows your business to operate smoothly, ensuring that you can cover expenses, pay employees, and invest in growth.
    - **Better Decision-Making:** With good financial habits, you have a clearer understanding of your financial situation, enabling you to make informed decisions.

**Keeping Credit Utilization Low**

Credit utilization refers to the percentage of your available credit that you're currently using. Keeping this percentage low is crucial for maintaining a healthy credit score.

**Why Low Credit Utilization Matters:**

- **Impact on Credit Score:** Credit utilization is one of the most significant factors in determining your credit score. High utilization can indicate that you're overly reliant on credit, which may be seen as a risk by lenders.
- **Financial Flexibility:** By keeping your utilization low, you maintain flexibility to access credit when needed without pushing your limits.

**How to Manage Credit Utilization:**

1. **Monitor Your Balances:**
   - Regularly check your credit card and line of credit balances to ensure you're not approaching your credit limit. Aim to keep your utilization below 30%, and ideally below 10%, of your total available credit.
2. **Increase Credit Limits:**
   - If possible, request a credit limit increase from your creditors. This can lower your utilization rate without requiring you to reduce spending. Just be careful not to view the higher limit as a reason to spend more.
3. **Pay Off Balances Early:**
   - Consider making multiple payments throughout the month to keep your balances low. This is especially helpful if you make frequent large purchases on your credit card.
4. **Use Multiple Cards:**
   - If you have multiple credit cards, spread your purchases across them rather than maxing out one card. This helps keep the utilization rate low on each individual card.

## Limiting Credit Inquiries

Every time you apply for new credit, a hard inquiry is made on your credit report, which can temporarily lower your credit score. Managing how often you apply for new credit is an essential aspect of maintaining a strong credit profile.

**Why Limiting Inquiries Matters:**

- **Impact on Credit Score:** Each hard inquiry can reduce your credit score by a few points. While this effect is temporary, multiple inquiries in a short period can add up and make you appear as a higher risk to lenders.
- **Signal of Financial Stability:** Applying for credit sparingly demonstrates to lenders that you're managing your finances well and aren't overly reliant on borrowing.

**How to Manage Credit Inquiries:**

1. **Plan Ahead:**
   - Before applying for credit, consider whether it's necessary and how it fits into your overall financial strategy. Only apply for credit when it aligns with your business goals.
2. **Research Before Applying:**
   - Do your homework before submitting a credit application. Many lenders offer pre-qualification processes that allow you to see potential offers without a hard inquiry. This can help you avoid unnecessary inquiries.
3. **Consolidate Applications:**

- If you need multiple credit products (like a loan and a credit card), try to apply for them within a short period, typically within 14-45 days, depending on the credit scoring model. This may help group the inquiries together, reducing their impact on your score.

4. **Monitor Your Credit:**
    - Regularly check your credit report to see how many inquiries have been made. If you notice unauthorized inquiries, report them immediately to the credit bureaus.

**Maintaining Accurate Financial Records**

Keeping accurate and up-to-date financial records is crucial for making informed decisions, securing financing, and ensuring that your business operates smoothly.

**Why Accurate Records Matter:**

- **Informed Decision-Making:** Accurate financial records provide a clear picture of your business's financial health, helping you make decisions about spending, investing, and expanding.
- **Compliance:** Proper record-keeping ensures that you comply with tax laws and other regulatory requirements, avoiding penalties and legal issues.
- **Ease of Financing:** When applying for loans or credit, lenders will require detailed financial records. Keeping your books in order makes the application process smoother and increases your chances of approval.

**How to Maintain Accurate Records:**

1. **Use Accounting Software:**
   - Invest in accounting software like QuickBooks, Wave, or FreshBooks. These tools help you track income, expenses, and cash flow, and generate financial statements with ease.
2. **Reconcile Accounts Regularly:**
   - Reconcile your bank and credit card statements monthly to ensure that your records match your actual balances. This helps catch errors or discrepancies early.
3. **Keep Receipts and Invoices:**
   - Maintain organized records of all business transactions, including receipts, invoices, and bank statements. This documentation is crucial for tax preparation and audits.
4. **Hire a Professional:**
   - If managing your books becomes too time-consuming or complex, consider hiring a bookkeeper or accountant. A professional can ensure that your records are accurate and that you're taking advantage of all available tax deductions.

**Creating and Sticking to a Budget**

A well-planned budget is the cornerstone of sound financial management. It helps you control spending, prioritize expenses, and ensure that your business stays on track financially.

**Why Budgeting Matters:**

- **Spending Control:** A budget helps you allocate your resources effectively, ensuring that you spend within your means and avoid unnecessary debt.
- **Financial Goals:** Budgeting allows you to set and achieve financial goals, such as saving for expansion, reducing debt, or increasing profitability.
- **Preparedness:** A budget helps you prepare for unexpected expenses and economic downturns, ensuring that your business remains resilient.

**How to Create and Stick to a Budget:**

1. **Assess Your Income and Expenses:**
    - Start by listing all sources of income and fixed expenses, such as rent, utilities, and payroll. Then, estimate variable expenses, like marketing and supplies.
2. **Set Financial Goals:**
    - Determine what you want to achieve with your budget, such as paying down debt, saving for a specific purpose, or increasing profitability.
3. **Allocate Funds:**
    - Distribute your income across different expense categories based on your priorities and goals. Ensure that you're setting aside funds for savings and unexpected costs.
4. **Review and Adjust Regularly:**
    - Review your budget monthly to track your progress and make adjustments as needed. If your business's financial situation changes, be flexible and update your budget accordingly.

5. **Use Budgeting Tools:**
   - Consider using budgeting tools or apps that can help you track your spending and stay within your budget. Many accounting software programs also include budgeting features.

**Developing a Savings Plan**

Having a savings plan is essential for managing cash flow, preparing for the future, and ensuring your business can weather financial challenges.

**Why Saving Matters:**

- **Emergency Fund:** A savings plan ensures you have funds set aside for emergencies, such as unexpected repairs, a sudden drop in sales, or other unforeseen expenses.
- **Investment Opportunities:** Having savings available allows you to take advantage of investment opportunities without needing to rely on credit or loans.
- **Financial Stability:** A robust savings plan contributes to your business's overall financial stability, helping you maintain cash flow and meet obligations even during tough times.

**How to Develop a Savings Plan:**

1. **Set Savings Goals:**
   - Determine how much you want to save each month or quarter. Set specific goals, such as building a three-month emergency fund or saving for a large purchase.
2. **Automate Savings:**

- Set up automatic transfers from your business checking account to your savings account. This ensures that a portion of your income is saved regularly without requiring manual effort.
3. **Choose the Right Savings Account:**
    - Consider opening a business savings account that offers a competitive interest rate. Some banks also offer money market accounts or certificates of deposit (CDs) for higher interest returns on larger balances.
4. **Monitor and Adjust:**
    - Regularly review your savings progress and adjust your plan as needed. If your business's income increases, consider increasing the amount you save each month.

**Free and Low-Cost Resources**

Here are some resources that can help you establish and maintain good financial habits:

- **Mint:** A free personal finance app that can also be used to track small business expenses, create budgets, and monitor savings goals.
- **QuickBooks:** Offers robust accounting and budgeting tools for businesses, including features for managing cash flow, tracking expenses, and saving for the future.
- **Wave:** A free accounting software designed for small businesses, offering features like invoicing, expense tracking, and financial reporting.

**Encouragement: Building a Foundation for Long-Term Success**

Good financial habits are the bedrock of a successful business. By consistently managing your credit utilization, limiting inquiries, maintaining accurate records, budgeting wisely, and saving for the future, you're not just keeping your business afloat—you're setting it up for sustainable growth and long-term success. Remember, the small, disciplined actions you take today will compound over time, leading to greater financial stability and opportunities tomorrow. Stay committed to these habits, and you'll build a strong, resilient business capable of thriving in any economic environment.

## Chapter 8: Advanced Tips for Growing Business Credit

By now, you've established a solid foundation for your business credit through good financial habits, timely payments, and prudent financial management. In this chapter, we'll dive into advanced strategies for growing your business credit even further. These tips are designed for businesses that have already established some credit and are looking to take it to the next level. We'll explore how to strategically scale your credit, maintain a perfect credit score, and leverage your credit for business growth.

**Why Growing Business Credit is Important**

1. **Access to Larger Financing:**

- **Bigger Opportunities:** As your business grows, so do your financial needs. Whether you're expanding operations, launching new products, or entering new markets, having strong business credit allows you to secure larger loans and credit lines.
- **Better Terms:** With a strong credit profile, you're more likely to receive favorable terms from lenders, including lower interest rates, higher credit limits, and more flexible repayment options.

2. **Strengthening Business Relationships:**
   - **Supplier Confidence:** Suppliers are more willing to offer better credit terms, such as net-60 or net-90, to businesses with strong credit. This can improve your cash flow and allow you to reinvest in your business.
   - **Investor Attraction:** A robust credit profile can make your business more attractive to investors, as it signals financial stability and growth potential.

3. **Enhancing Business Resilience:**
   - **Weathering Economic Downturns:** A strong credit profile provides a financial cushion during tough economic times, ensuring that your business can continue to operate smoothly even when cash flow is tight.
   - **Strategic Flexibility:** Having access to ample credit allows you to be more agile in responding to opportunities or challenges, giving your business a competitive edge.

**Scaling Your Credit**

As your business grows, scaling your credit becomes a strategic priority. Here's how to do it effectively:

**1. Gradually Increase Credit Limits:**

- **Request Higher Limits:** As you build a history of on-time payments and responsible credit use, periodically request higher credit limits from your lenders. This not only increases your available credit but also lowers your credit utilization ratio.
- **Diversify Credit Sources:** Don't rely on a single credit line or lender. Apply for additional credit lines with other institutions, such as business credit cards, vendor accounts, or lines of credit. This diversification helps strengthen your overall credit profile.

**2. Maintain a Low Credit Utilization Ratio:**

- **Utilization Strategy:** Aim to keep your credit utilization below 30%, and ideally below 10%, across all your credit accounts. This demonstrates financial discipline and positively impacts your credit score.
- **Use Multiple Accounts:** Spread your expenses across multiple credit accounts rather than maxing out a single one. This helps maintain a low utilization ratio on each account.

**3. Establish Long-Term Trade Lines:**

- **Build Relationships with Key Vendors:** Establish long-term trade lines with vendors who report to business credit bureaus. Prioritize working with vendors who offer favorable terms and are likely to grow alongside your business.

- **Negotiate Terms:** As your business credit improves, negotiate better terms with your vendors, such as extended payment periods or higher credit limits. This not only benefits your cash flow but also strengthens your credit profile.

4. **Secure a Business Loan for Strategic Investments:**

- **Use Loans for Growth:** Consider taking out a business loan for strategic investments, such as purchasing new equipment, expanding your facilities, or launching a major marketing campaign. Successfully managing a larger loan demonstrates your business's creditworthiness and ability to handle significant financial responsibilities.
- **Leverage Collateral:** If possible, use business assets as collateral to secure better loan terms. This reduces the risk for lenders and can result in lower interest rates and higher loan amounts.

**Maintaining a Perfect Credit Score**

Once you've established strong business credit, the next step is to maintain it. Here's how to keep your credit score in top shape:

1. **Continue Making On-Time Payments:**

- **Never Miss a Payment:** Payment history is the most important factor in your credit score. Continue to make all payments on time, even as your business grows and your financial obligations increase.
- **Automate Payments:** To ensure you never miss a payment, automate as many of your payments as possible. Set up reminders for manual payments to avoid any delays.

2. **Monitor Your Credit Regularly:**
   - **Regular Credit Checks:** Regularly review your business credit reports from all major bureaus (Dun & Bradstreet, Experian, Equifax). This helps you stay informed about your credit status and catch any errors or discrepancies early.
   - **Use Monitoring Services:** Consider using credit monitoring services like Nav or CreditSignal to receive alerts about changes to your credit profile and to track your credit score over time.

3. **Avoid Unnecessary Credit Inquiries:**
   - **Be Strategic About New Credit:** Only apply for new credit when it's necessary and aligns with your business goals. Multiple credit inquiries in a short period can lower your credit score.
   - **Pre-Qualification Offers:** Look for lenders who offer pre-qualification, which allows you to see potential offers without a hard inquiry on your credit report.

4. **Keep Your Debt Levels Manageable:**
   - **Debt Management:** Avoid taking on more debt than your business can comfortably repay. High levels of debt can strain your cash flow and increase your risk of default, negatively impacting your credit score.
   - **Pay Off Debt Early:** If your cash flow allows, consider paying off loans or credit lines early. This reduces your debt load and can improve your credit score.

**Leveraging Business Credit for Growth**

Once your business credit is strong, you can leverage it for strategic growth. Here's how:

1. **Invest in Business Expansion:**

   - **New Markets:** Use your strong credit profile to secure financing for entering new markets or launching new product lines. Expanding your business's reach can lead to increased revenue and long-term growth.
   - **Acquire New Assets:** Consider using credit to invest in new assets, such as real estate, equipment, or technology. These investments can increase your business's efficiency and profitability.

2. **Secure Better Supplier Terms:**

   - **Negotiate with Suppliers:** Leverage your strong credit profile to negotiate better terms with suppliers, such as extended payment periods, bulk discounts, or exclusive deals. This can improve your cash flow and reduce costs.
   - **Expand Vendor Relationships:** Establish relationships with new vendors who offer favorable credit terms and products or services that align with your business needs.

3. **Build Strategic Partnerships:**

   - **Joint Ventures:** Strong credit can make your business an attractive partner for joint ventures or strategic alliances. Use your creditworthiness to form partnerships that can drive growth and innovation.

- **Attract Investors:** A robust credit profile can also attract investors who are looking for stable and financially sound businesses to invest in. Use this opportunity to secure funding for larger projects or expansion plans.

4. **Prepare for Future Financing Needs:**
    - **Plan for Growth:** As your business grows, your financing needs will evolve. Continuously evaluate your business's financial situation and credit profile to ensure you're prepared to secure the necessary capital for future projects.
    - **Build Relationships with Lenders:** Establish and maintain strong relationships with multiple lenders. Having established relationships can make it easier to secure financing when you need it, often with better terms.

**Free and Low-Cost Resources**

Here are some resources that can help you grow and maintain your business credit:

- **Nav:** Offers free and paid plans for monitoring and improving your business credit, with personalized insights and recommendations.
- **Dun & Bradstreet CreditBuilder:** A service that helps you build and monitor your D&B credit profile, with options for adding trade references.
- **Score:** Provides free mentoring and resources for small businesses, including guidance on managing and leveraging business credit for growth.

**Encouragement: Elevating Your Business to New Heights**

Growing your business credit is about more than just increasing your financial options—it's about positioning your business for long-term success and resilience. By strategically scaling your credit, maintaining a perfect credit score, and leveraging your financial strength for growth, you're setting your business up for greater opportunities and a brighter future. Remember, the work you put into building and maintaining your credit is an investment in your business's continued success. Keep pushing forward, stay disciplined, and watch as your business reaches new heights.

## Chapter 9: Building Credit with Microloans and Community Lenders

As you continue to grow your business and credit profile, you may find that traditional financing options aren't always the best fit, especially if you're a small or newer business. Microloans and community lenders offer an alternative path to building credit and securing the funds you need to expand. In this chapter, we'll explore how these options work, how to apply for them, and how they can help strengthen your business credit.

**Understanding Microloans and Community Lenders**

1. **What Are Microloans?**
    - **Small Loan Amounts:** Microloans are small, short-term loans typically offered to small businesses, startups, or entrepreneurs

who may not qualify for traditional bank loans. Loan amounts usually range from $500 to $50,000.
    - **Flexible Terms:** Microloans often have more flexible terms than traditional loans, with lower interest rates and longer repayment periods.
    - **Focus on Community Development:** Many microloan programs are designed to support underserved communities, women-owned businesses, minority-owned businesses, and businesses in rural areas.
2. **What Are Community Lenders?**
    - **Local Focus:** Community lenders, such as Community Development Financial Institutions (CDFIs), are nonprofit organizations that provide financial services to underserved markets. They focus on supporting local businesses and community development.
    - **Personalized Service:** Community lenders often offer personalized support, including financial education, business mentoring, and technical assistance, making them a valuable resource for new or small businesses.
3. **Benefits of Microloans and Community Lenders:**
    - **Easier Qualification:** These loans often have less stringent credit requirements, making them accessible to businesses with limited credit history.
    - **Credit Building:** Successfully repaying a microloan can help establish or improve your business credit profile, making it easier to qualify for larger loans in the future.

- **Community Impact:** By working with community lenders, you're contributing to the local economy and supporting community development.

**How to Apply for Microloans**

Applying for a microloan involves several steps, but the process is generally more straightforward than applying for a traditional bank loan:

**1. Identify the Right Lender:**

- **Research Local Options:** Start by researching microloan programs and community lenders in your area. Many CDFIs have specific geographic or demographic focuses, so finding a lender that aligns with your business's needs is important.
- **Consider Online Lenders:** Some online platforms, such as Kiva and Accion, offer microloans with flexible terms and accessible application processes.

**2. Prepare Your Application:**

- **Business Plan:** Even for a microloan, you'll need a solid business plan that outlines your goals, financial projections, and how you plan to use the loan funds.
- **Financial Documents:** Gather financial statements, tax returns, and other relevant documents that demonstrate your business's financial health.
- **Personal Credit:** While microloan lenders may consider your business credit, they often place more emphasis on your personal credit, especially if your business is new.

**3. Submit the Application:**

- **Complete the Form:** Fill out the loan application, providing detailed and accurate information about your business and its financial situation.
- **Include Supporting Documents:** Attach all required documents, including your business plan and financial statements.
- **Follow Up:** After submitting your application, follow up with the lender to ensure they have everything they need and to demonstrate your commitment to securing the loan.

**4. Use the Funds Wisely:**

- **Stick to the Plan:** Once you receive the loan, use the funds exactly as outlined in your business plan. This not only ensures you meet your goals but also builds trust with the lender.
- **Make Timely Payments:** Repay the loan on time to build your credit profile and strengthen your relationship with the lender.

**The Role of Microloans in Building Business Credit**

Microloans can play a pivotal role in building your business credit, especially if you're just starting out:

**1. Establishing Credit History:**

- **Initial Credit Building:** If your business has little to no credit history, a microloan can help you establish that history. As you make timely payments, your business credit score will begin to grow.

**2. Improving Credit Score:**

- **Boosting Your Profile:** Regular, on-time payments on a microloan are reported to credit bureaus, positively impacting your credit score. This can make it easier to qualify for larger loans or credit lines in the future.

3. **Building Relationships:**

- **Lender Trust:** Successfully managing a microloan builds trust with lenders, which can lead to better terms and higher credit limits in the future. It also strengthens your overall financial network, opening doors to additional opportunities.

**Free and Low-Cost Resources**

Here are some resources that can help you explore microloans and community lenders:

- **SBA Microloan Program:** Provides small loans through intermediary lenders to help small businesses and certain nonprofit child care centers start and expand.
- **Kiva:** An online platform offering microloans with 0% interest to small businesses and entrepreneurs.
- **Accion:** A nonprofit organization providing microloans and support services to small businesses in the United States.

**Encouragement: Leveraging Community Resources for Growth**

Microloans and community lenders are more than just financial resources—they are partners in your business journey. By leveraging these resources, you're not only securing the funds you need but also building relationships that can support your business's growth and success. Remember, every step you take to build your credit, whether large or small, is a step toward a stronger, more resilient business. Keep pushing forward, and use the opportunities available to you to create the future you envision for your business.

## Chapter 10: The Role of Business Credit Scores

Your business credit score is a vital component of your overall financial health. It influences everything from loan approvals to supplier relationships and even your ability to lease property. In this chapter, we'll explore the different types of business credit scores, how they're calculated, and how you can maintain and improve your scores.

**Understanding Business Credit Scores**

1. **What is a Business Credit Score?**
   - **Overview:** A business credit score is a numerical representation of your business's creditworthiness, based on its financial history and behavior. It's similar to a personal credit score but focuses solely on your business's financial activities.
   - **Purpose:** Lenders, suppliers, and other financial partners use your business credit score to assess the risk of extending credit to your business.
2. **Types of Business Credit Scores:**

- **Dun & Bradstreet PAYDEX Score:** Ranges from 0 to 100 and is based on your business's payment history with suppliers and creditors. A score of 80 or above is considered strong.
- **Experian Intelliscore Plus:** Ranges from 1 to 100, combining your business credit history with public records and demographic information. A score of 76 or above is considered good.
- **Equifax Business Credit Risk Score:** Ranges from 101 to 992 and assesses the likelihood of your business becoming delinquent on payments. A score above 700 is generally favorable.
- **FICO SBSS Score:** Ranges from 0 to 300 and is used by lenders to evaluate small business creditworthiness, particularly for SBA loans. A score of 160 or higher is typically required for approval.

3. **Why Business Credit Scores Matter:**
    - **Access to Credit:** A higher credit score increases your chances of being approved for loans, lines of credit, and other financing options, often with better terms.
    - **Supplier Relationships:** Suppliers may offer better payment terms, such as extended net terms, to businesses with strong credit scores.
    - **Business Opportunities:** A solid credit score can enhance your reputation with potential partners, investors, and even customers.

**How Business Credit Scores Are Calculated**

Business credit scores are calculated based on several factors, including:

1. **Payment History:**

   - **Timeliness:** The most critical factor is whether you pay your bills on time. Late payments or delinquencies can significantly lower your score.
   - **Payment Patterns:** Regularly paying early or on time strengthens your score, while inconsistent payment patterns can weaken it.

2. **Credit Utilization:**

   - **Credit Usage:** The amount of credit you're using relative to your available credit limit. High utilization can indicate financial stress and negatively impact your score.
   - **Managing Balances:** Keeping your credit utilization low, ideally below 30%, is crucial for maintaining a strong score.

3. **Length of Credit History:**

   - **Account Age:** The longer your business credit history, the better. Older accounts with positive payment histories contribute more favorably to your score.
   - **New Credit Accounts:** Opening several new accounts in a short period can lower the average age of your credit accounts and negatively impact your score.

4. **Credit Mix:**

- **Diverse Credit Sources:** A mix of credit types, such as loans, credit cards, and vendor accounts, demonstrates that your business can manage different forms of credit responsibly.

5. Public Records:

- **Legal Filings:** Bankruptcies, liens, and judgments can severely impact your business credit score. It's essential to avoid these issues or resolve them quickly if they arise.

How to Improve and Maintain High Credit Scores

1. Monitor Your Credit Regularly:

- **Regular Checks:** Review your business credit reports regularly from all major bureaus (Dun & Bradstreet, Experian, Equifax) to ensure accuracy and stay informed of any changes.
- **Dispute Errors:** If you find inaccuracies on your credit report, dispute them promptly to avoid any negative impact on your score.

2. Pay Bills on Time:

- **Timely Payments:** Always pay your bills on time or early. Even one late payment can harm your credit score.
- **Automate Payments:** Set up automatic payments for recurring bills to ensure they're always paid on time.

3. Manage Credit Utilization:

- **Keep Utilization Low:** Aim to keep your credit utilization below 30% of your available credit. Spread expenses across multiple accounts if necessary.
- **Increase Credit Limits:** Request higher credit limits from your creditors to lower your utilization ratio, but avoid the temptation to overspend.

4. **Build Long-Term Credit Relationships:**

- **Maintain Older Accounts:** Keep older credit accounts open and active to benefit from their long history of positive payments.
- **Diversify Credit Types:** Use different types of credit, such as loans, credit cards, and vendor accounts, to build a robust credit profile.

**Free and Low-Cost Resources**

Here are some resources that can help you monitor and improve your business credit scores:

- **Nav:** Offers free and paid tools for monitoring your business credit scores from all major bureaus, with personalized advice on how to improve your scores.
- **Dun & Bradstreet CreditSignal:** A free service that alerts you to changes in your D&B credit file, helping you stay proactive in managing your score.
- **Experian Business Credit Reports:** Provides affordable access to your business credit report, along with credit monitoring services.

**Encouragement: Taking Control of Your Business's Financial Health**

Your business credit score is more than just a number—it's a reflection of your business's financial health, responsibility, and potential for growth. By understanding how these scores are calculated and taking steps to improve and maintain them, you're not just safeguarding your business today—you're setting it up for long-term success. Stay diligent, make informed decisions, and continue building a strong, resilient business credit profile that will support your goals and aspirations for years to come.

## Chapter 11: Creating a Business Plan and Financial Projections

A well-crafted business plan and accurate financial projections are critical tools for securing financing, attracting investors, and guiding your business's growth. In this chapter, we'll discuss how to create a comprehensive business plan and develop financial projections that align with your business goals.

**Why a Business Plan Matters**

1. **Roadmap for Success:**
    - **Guidance:** A business plan serves as a roadmap for your business, outlining your goals, strategies, and the steps you'll take to achieve them. It helps you stay focused and on track as your business grows.
    - **Decision-Making:** By providing a clear picture of your business's future, a business plan helps you make informed decisions about operations, finances, and growth opportunities.

2. **Securing Financing:**
   - **Investor Confidence:** Investors and lenders want to see that you have a clear plan for your business's future. A well-prepared business plan demonstrates that you've thought through all aspects of your business and are prepared for success.
   - **Loan Applications:** Many lenders require a business plan as part of the loan application process. A strong plan increases your chances of approval and may help you secure better terms.
3. **Attracting Partners:**
   - **Partnership Opportunities:** A detailed business plan can help attract potential partners, such as suppliers, distributors, or strategic alliances, by showing that your business is well-organized and poised for growth.

**Components of a Business Plan**

A comprehensive business plan typically includes the following sections:

**1. Executive Summary:**

- **Overview:** A brief summary of your business, including your mission statement, products or services, target market, and financial goals. This section should be concise but compelling, as it's often the first thing investors or lenders will read.

**2. Company Description:**

- **Business Details:** Provide detailed information about your business, including its history, structure, location, and the products or services you offer. Highlight what makes your business unique and how it meets the needs of your target market.

3. **Market Analysis:**

- **Industry Overview:** Analyze the market in which your business operates, including industry trends, target market demographics, and competitive analysis. This section should demonstrate your understanding of the market and your business's position within it.

4. **Organization and Management:**

- **Business Structure:** Outline your business's organizational structure, including ownership, management team, and key roles. Include bios of key team members, highlighting their experience and expertise.
- **Legal Structure:** Describe your business's legal structure (LLC, S-Corp, etc.) and explain why this structure is best for your business.

5. **Products or Services:**

- **Offerings:** Provide detailed descriptions of the products or services you offer, including how they are produced or delivered, their pricing, and their unique value proposition.
- **Development:** If applicable, include information on the development stage of your products or services and any future plans for new offerings.

### 6. Marketing and Sales Strategy:

- **Marketing Plan:** Outline your strategy for reaching your target market, including your marketing channels, advertising tactics, and promotional activities.
- **Sales Strategy:** Describe your sales process, including how you plan to generate leads, close sales, and build customer relationships.

### 7. Financial Projections:

- **Revenue Projections:** Provide detailed financial projections, including revenue forecasts, profit and loss statements, cash flow projections, and balance sheets for the next three to five years.
- **Break-Even Analysis:** Include a break-even analysis that shows when your business will become profitable.
- **Funding Requirements:** If you're seeking financing, outline the amount of funding you need, how you'll use it, and how it will impact your business's growth.

### 8. Appendix:

- **Supporting Documents:** Include any additional documents that support your business plan, such as resumes, legal agreements, product photos, or market research data.

### Creating Financial Projections

Financial projections are a key component of your business plan. They provide a detailed picture of your business's financial future and help you set realistic goals:

1. **Revenue Projections:**
   - **Sales Forecast:** Estimate your expected sales over the next three to five years, based on market research, historical data, and your marketing strategy.
   - **Revenue Streams:** Identify all potential revenue streams, including product sales, service fees, subscriptions, or licensing.

2. **Profit and Loss Statement:**
   - **Income Statement:** Create a profit and loss (P&L) statement that projects your business's income, expenses, and net profit over the next three to five years.
   - **Expense Categories:** Break down your expenses into categories such as cost of goods sold, operating expenses, and taxes.

3. **Cash Flow Projections:**
   - **Cash Flow Forecast:** Estimate your business's cash inflows and outflows, including sales, expenses, loan repayments, and investments. This helps you ensure that your business has enough cash to cover its obligations and invest in growth.

4. **Balance Sheet Projections:**
   - **Assets and Liabilities:** Project your business's assets, liabilities, and equity over the next three to five years. This provides a snapshot of your business's financial position and helps you track its growth.

5. **Break-Even Analysis:**

- **Break-Even Point:** Calculate the point at which your business's revenue will cover its expenses, indicating when your business will start generating a profit.

**Free and Low-Cost Resources**

Here are some resources to help you create a business plan and financial projections:

- **SBA Business Plan Tool:** A free, step-by-step guide to creating a business plan, provided by the U.S. Small Business Administration.
- **Score Business Plan Template:** A free, downloadable business plan template from SCORE, complete with instructions and examples.
- **LivePlan:** A paid business planning software that offers tools for creating professional business plans and financial projections.

**Encouragement: Planning for Success**

A well-crafted business plan and accurate financial projections are essential tools for navigating the challenges and opportunities that lie ahead. By taking the time to plan, you're not just preparing for today—you're setting the stage for your business's future success. Whether you're seeking financing, attracting partners, or simply guiding your business toward growth, your plan is your blueprint for achieving your goals. Stay focused, be realistic, and let your plan guide you toward the success you envision.

## Chapter 12: Understanding Business Insurance

Business insurance is a crucial aspect of protecting your business and its assets. Whether you're just starting out or expanding, understanding the types of insurance available and what they cover can help you safeguard your business against potential risks. In this chapter, we'll explore the basics of business insurance, the different types of coverage available, and how to choose the right insurance for your business.

**Why Business Insurance is Important**

1. **Protecting Your Assets:**
   - **Financial Security:** Business insurance helps protect your business's physical and financial assets, such as property, equipment, and inventory, from unexpected events like theft, fire, or natural disasters.
   - **Liability Coverage:** Liability insurance protects your business from claims of injury or property damage caused by your products, services, or operations.
2. **Legal Requirements:**
   - **Compliance:** Some types of business insurance, such as workers' compensation and commercial auto insurance, are legally required in many states. Failing to carry the necessary insurance can result in fines, penalties, or legal action.
   - **Contractual Obligations:** Many contracts with clients, vendors, or landlords may require you to carry specific types of

insurance, such as general liability or professional liability insurance.

3. **Business Continuity:**
   - **Disaster Recovery:** Insurance can help your business recover from a disaster by covering the costs of repairs, replacement, and lost income, ensuring that your business can continue operating.
   - **Employee Protection:** Health insurance, workers' compensation, and other employee benefits help protect your workforce, contributing to employee satisfaction and retention.

**Types of Business Insurance**

There are several types of business insurance to consider, each designed to protect different aspects of your business:

**1. General Liability Insurance:**

- **Coverage:** Protects your business from claims of bodily injury, property damage, and personal injury (such as libel or slander) that occur as a result of your business operations.
- **Importance:** This is the most basic form of business insurance and is essential for protecting your business from common risks.

**2. Professional Liability Insurance:**

- **Coverage:** Also known as errors and omissions (E&O) insurance, this coverage protects your business from claims of negligence, mistakes, or failure to deliver promised services.

- **Importance:** Particularly important for service-based businesses, professional liability insurance helps protect against lawsuits related to the quality of your work.

3. **Property Insurance:**
   - **Coverage:** Covers damage to your business's physical assets, such as buildings, equipment, and inventory, caused by events like fire, theft, or vandalism.
   - **Importance:** Property insurance is crucial for protecting your business's physical assets and ensuring you can recover quickly from a loss.

4. **Workers' Compensation Insurance:**
   - **Coverage:** Provides benefits to employees who are injured or become ill as a result of their job. This insurance covers medical expenses, lost wages, and disability benefits.
   - **Importance:** Workers' compensation is legally required in most states and helps protect both your employees and your business from the financial impact of workplace injuries.

5. **Commercial Auto Insurance:**
   - **Coverage:** Covers vehicles owned or used by your business for work-related activities, protecting against damage, theft, and liability in the event of an accident.
   - **Importance:** If your business uses vehicles for deliveries, transportation, or any other purpose, commercial auto insurance is essential.

**6. Business Interruption Insurance:**

- **Coverage:** Covers lost income and operating expenses if your business is forced to close temporarily due to a covered event, such as a natural disaster or fire.
- **Importance:** Business interruption insurance helps ensure that your business can continue to meet financial obligations even if operations are temporarily halted.

**7. Cyber Liability Insurance:**

- **Coverage:** Protects your business from the financial impact of data breaches, cyberattacks, and other online threats. Coverage may include legal fees, notification costs, and recovery of lost data.
- **Importance:** As businesses increasingly rely on digital operations, cyber liability insurance is becoming essential for protecting against the risks of cybercrime.

**8. Product Liability Insurance:**

- **Coverage:** Protects your business from claims related to injury or damage caused by a product you manufacture, distribute, or sell.
- **Importance:** For businesses that create or sell physical products, product liability insurance is crucial for protecting against the financial impact of product-related lawsuits.

**How to Choose the Right Insurance for Your Business**

Choosing the right insurance coverage depends on several factors, including the nature of your business, the risks you face, and your budget:

1. **Assess Your Risks:**
   - **Identify Potential Hazards:** Consider the specific risks your business faces, such as the potential for property damage, liability claims, employee injuries, or cyber threats.
   - **Evaluate Financial Impact:** Assess how each risk could impact your business financially and determine which risks you're most concerned about.

2. **Determine Your Coverage Needs:**
   - **Basic Coverage:** Start with essential coverage like general liability and property insurance, which protect against common risks.
   - **Industry-Specific Coverage:** Consider additional coverage that's specific to your industry, such as professional liability for service businesses or product liability for manufacturers.

3. **Compare Insurance Providers:**
   - **Shop Around:** Get quotes from multiple insurance providers to compare coverage options, premiums, and customer service. Look for providers with experience in your industry.
   - **Consider Bundling:** Some insurers offer discounts if you bundle multiple types of coverage, such as general liability and property insurance, into a single policy.

4. **Review Policy Details:**

- **Understand the Terms:** Carefully review the terms of each policy, including coverage limits, exclusions, and deductibles. Make sure you understand what is and isn't covered.
- **Consult an Agent:** If you're unsure about your insurance needs, consider consulting an insurance agent or broker who can help you choose the right coverage for your business.

### 5. Reevaluate Annually:

- **Update Your Coverage:** As your business grows and evolves, your insurance needs may change. Review your coverage annually to ensure it still meets your needs and adjust as necessary.

**Free and Low-Cost Resources**

Here are some resources to help you choose and manage your business insurance:

- **SBA Insurance Guide:** A comprehensive guide from the Small Business Administration that covers the basics of business insurance and how to choose the right coverage.
- **Insureon:** An online platform that helps small businesses compare insurance quotes from top providers.
- **Score:** Provides free mentoring and resources on business insurance and risk management.

**Encouragement: Protecting Your Business for the Future**

Business insurance is an essential investment in your business's future. By understanding your risks and choosing the right coverage, you're not just protecting your assets—you're safeguarding your business's potential for growth and success. Remember, insurance is about more than just compliance—it's about ensuring that your business can weather any storm and continue to thrive. Stay informed, choose wisely, and take the necessary steps to protect the business you've worked so hard to build.

## Chapter 13: Building Business Credit Through Leasing

Leasing is an often-overlooked strategy for building business credit. By leasing equipment, vehicles, or office space, you can establish a credit history, conserve cash, and gain access to the resources your business needs to grow. In this chapter, we'll explore the benefits of leasing, how it impacts your credit, and how to choose the right leasing options for your business.

**Why Leasing Can Build Credit**

1. **Establishing Payment History:**
   - **Regular Payments:** Just like loans or credit cards, leasing agreements require regular payments. These payments are often reported to credit bureaus, helping to build your business credit history.
   - **Timeliness:** Consistently making on-time lease payments demonstrates financial responsibility, which positively impacts your credit score.
2. **Preserving Cash Flow:**

- **Lower Upfront Costs:** Leasing allows you to acquire expensive equipment or assets with lower upfront costs compared to purchasing. This helps conserve cash flow for other business needs.
- **Predictable Expenses:** Lease payments are typically fixed, making it easier to budget and manage your cash flow.

3. **Flexibility and Scalability:**
   - **Upgrade Options:** Leasing often provides the flexibility to upgrade to newer equipment or technology as your business grows, without the financial burden of owning outdated assets.
   - **End-of-Lease Choices:** At the end of a lease term, you may have the option to purchase the leased asset, renew the lease, or lease new equipment, allowing your business to adapt to changing needs.

**Types of Leases**

There are several types of leases to consider, each with its own benefits and considerations:

**1. Operating Lease:**

- **Overview:** An operating lease is a short-term lease where the lessor (the owner of the asset) retains ownership, and the lessee (your business) uses the asset for a set period.
- **Benefits:** Lower monthly payments, no ownership responsibility, and the ability to upgrade equipment at the end of the lease term.
- **Considerations:** At the end of the lease, you'll need to return the asset or negotiate a new lease.

## 2. Capital Lease:

- **Overview:** A capital lease, also known as a finance lease, is a long-term lease where the lessee assumes many of the rights and responsibilities of ownership. The asset is recorded as an asset and a liability on your balance sheet.
- **Benefits:** Potential tax benefits, fixed payments, and the option to purchase the asset at the end of the lease term.
- **Considerations:** Higher monthly payments and the responsibility for maintenance and insurance.

## 3. Equipment Lease:

- **Overview:** An equipment lease is a specific type of lease used for acquiring machinery, vehicles, or other business equipment. It can be structured as either an operating or capital lease.
- **Benefits:** Access to essential equipment without the upfront costs of purchasing, with the flexibility to upgrade or replace equipment as needed.
- **Considerations:** Ensure the lease terms align with the expected lifespan and usage of the equipment.

## 4. Real Estate Lease:

- **Overview:** A real estate lease involves renting office space, retail space, or other commercial property for your business operations. This is typically structured as an operating lease.
- **Benefits:** Flexibility to relocate or expand without the commitment of owning property, with predictable rental payments.

- **Considerations:** Lease terms, such as length and renewal options, should be carefully negotiated to meet your business needs.

### How Leasing Impacts Your Credit

Leasing can have a positive impact on your business credit if managed responsibly:

**1. Building Credit History:**

- **Reported Payments:** Many leasing companies report payment history to business credit bureaus. Making timely lease payments builds your credit history and improves your credit score.
- **Diverse Credit Profile:** Leasing adds diversity to your credit profile by showing that your business can manage different types of financial obligations.

**2. Impact on Credit Utilization:**

- **Lower Utilization:** Since lease payments are typically lower than loan payments for similar assets, leasing can help keep your credit utilization low, positively impacting your credit score.

**3. Potential Credit Risks:**

- **Late Payments:** Late or missed lease payments can harm your credit score, just like any other form of credit. Ensure that you can meet your lease obligations before entering into an agreement.
- **Lease Default:** Defaulting on a lease can result in repossession of the leased asset, legal action, and a negative impact on your credit score.

## Choosing the Right Leasing Options

Choosing the right leasing options for your business involves several considerations:

### 1. Assess Your Needs:

- **Identify Essential Assets:** Determine which assets are essential for your business operations and whether leasing or purchasing is the best option.
- **Evaluate Usage:** Consider how long you'll need the asset and how frequently it will be used. Short-term or high-turnover assets may be better suited for leasing.

### 2. Compare Leasing Companies:

- **Research Providers:** Compare leasing companies based on their reputation, customer service, and lease terms. Look for providers that report payments to credit bureaus.
- **Negotiate Terms:** Negotiate lease terms that align with your business's financial situation, including payment schedules, maintenance responsibilities, and end-of-lease options.

### 3. Review Lease Agreements Carefully:

- **Understand the Terms:** Read the lease agreement thoroughly, paying close attention to terms like payment amounts, duration, renewal options, and any penalties for early termination.

- **Seek Professional Advice:** If you're unsure about the terms of a lease agreement, consult with a financial advisor or attorney to ensure it's in your best interest.

**4. Plan for the End of the Lease:**

- **End-of-Lease Options:** Consider your options at the end of the lease term, such as purchasing the asset, renewing the lease, or returning the asset. Plan ahead to avoid any surprises or disruptions to your business operations.

**Free and Low-Cost Resources**

Here are some resources to help you explore leasing options and manage your lease agreements:

- **LeaseQ:** An online platform that connects businesses with leasing companies and provides quotes for equipment leases.
- **Nav Leasing Guide:** A comprehensive guide to equipment leasing and how it can help build your business credit.
- **Small Business Development Centers (SBDCs):** Offer free consulting and resources on leasing, financing, and other business needs.

**Encouragement: Leveraging Leasing for Growth**

Leasing is a powerful tool for growing your business while building your credit. By choosing the right leasing options and managing your leases responsibly, you can access the resources you need to expand, innovate, and thrive. Remember, leasing isn't just about acquiring assets—it's about strategically positioning your business for long-term success. Stay informed, choose wisely, and let leasing be a part of your journey toward greater financial strength and business growth.

## Chapter 14: Case Studies and Success Stories

Learning from the experiences of others can be incredibly valuable as you work to build and grow your business credit. In this chapter, we'll explore real-life case studies and success stories from businesses that have successfully built strong credit profiles, secured financing, and achieved their growth goals. These stories will provide practical insights, lessons learned, and inspiration for your own business journey.

### Case Study 1: From Startup to Scale-Up

**Background:**

- **Business Type:** E-commerce retail
- **Founder:** Sarah, a first-time entrepreneur with a passion for handmade jewelry
- **Challenge:** Limited startup capital and no established business credit

**Journey:**

- **Starting Small:** Sarah began her business with a small personal loan and bootstrapped her way to early success by selling her jewelry at local markets and online.
- **Building Vendor Credit:** She established vendor accounts with suppliers who offered net-30 terms and reported payments to business credit bureaus. By consistently paying her invoices on time, she quickly built a positive credit history.
- **Expanding with a Business Credit Card:** After six months of consistent vendor payments, Sarah applied for a business credit card. She used the card responsibly, keeping her utilization low and paying the balance in full each month.
- **Securing a Business Loan:** With a strong credit profile, Sarah was able to secure a small business loan to fund a major marketing campaign and expand her product line. The campaign was a success, leading to increased sales and profitability.

**Outcome:**

- **Credit Score Growth:** Over the course of two years, Sarah's business credit score grew from zero to over 80 on the Dun & Bradstreet PAYDEX scale.
- **Business Expansion:** The combination of vendor credit, a business credit card, and a small business loan allowed Sarah to scale her business, open a physical store, and hire additional staff.
- **Lessons Learned:** Sarah emphasizes the importance of starting small, paying bills on time, and using credit wisely. She attributes her success to disciplined financial management and a willingness to invest in her business's growth.

## Case Study 2: Navigating Economic Challenges

**Background:**

- **Business Type:** Restaurant
- **Owner:** John, a seasoned restaurateur with two successful locations
- **Challenge:** Managing cash flow during an economic downturn

**Journey:**

- **Leveraging Existing Credit:** John had already built strong relationships with suppliers and had a solid business credit profile. When the economy took a downturn, he leveraged his credit to negotiate extended payment terms with suppliers, helping to ease cash flow pressures.
- **Applying for an SBA Loan:** John applied for an SBA loan to cover operating expenses and payroll during the slow period. His strong credit score and detailed business plan helped him secure the loan with favorable terms.
- **Using Business Insurance:** John's business interruption insurance helped cover lost income during a temporary closure, allowing him to maintain operations and keep his staff employed.

**Outcome:**

- **Resilience:** John's proactive approach to managing his business credit and leveraging available resources allowed his restaurants to weather the economic downturn without significant losses.

- **Credit Score Maintenance:** Despite the challenges, John maintained his business's credit score by making timely payments on all obligations, including the SBA loan.
- **Lessons Learned:** John highlights the importance of maintaining strong relationships with suppliers and lenders, as well as having a contingency plan in place. He credits his ability to navigate the downturn to his disciplined approach to financial management and credit maintenance.

**Case Study 3: The Power of Community Lenders**

Background:

- **Business Type:** Tech startup
- **Founder:** Maria, an experienced software developer with a vision for a new app
- **Challenge:** Limited access to traditional financing due to the startup's early stage

Journey:

- **Seeking Alternative Financing:** Maria struggled to secure traditional bank loans due to her startup's lack of revenue history. She turned to a local community lender that offered microloans and support for tech entrepreneurs.
- **Building Credit with Microloans:** Maria used a microloan to fund the initial development of her app. The lender reported her payments to business credit bureaus, helping her establish a credit history.

- **Securing Venture Capital:** With a growing credit profile and a working prototype of her app, Maria attracted the attention of venture capital investors. The microloan had not only provided the funds she needed but also demonstrated her financial responsibility.

Outcome:

- **Credit Score Establishment:** The microloan helped Maria build a business credit score from scratch, positioning her startup for future financing opportunities.
- **Investor Confidence:** The combination of a solid business plan, a working product, and a positive credit history helped Maria secure venture capital funding to scale her app.
- **Lessons Learned:** Maria's experience underscores the value of exploring alternative financing options and the importance of building business credit from the start. She advises other entrepreneurs to be open to community lenders and microloans as a pathway to growth.

**Free and Low-Cost Resources**

Here are some resources that can help you learn from others' experiences and apply those lessons to your own business:

- **Score Success Stories:** Read success stories from small business owners who have benefited from SCORE's mentoring and resources.
- **BiggerPockets Forums:** Join a community of entrepreneurs and investors sharing their experiences and lessons learned in business credit, financing, and growth.

- **SBA Learning Center:** Access free courses and resources on business financing, credit, and management, with real-world examples and case studies.

**Encouragement: Learning from Success**

The stories and experiences of others can be powerful motivators as you work to build and grow your business credit. By learning from their successes—and their challenges—you can gain valuable insights that will help you navigate your own journey. Remember, every business has its unique path, but the principles of discipline, perseverance, and smart financial management are universal. Keep learning, stay inspired, and continue working toward the success you envision for your business.

## Chapter 15: Networking and Mentorship

Building strong business credit is not just about financial management—it's also about building relationships. Networking and mentorship are powerful tools that can help you navigate the complexities of business credit, connect with valuable resources, and gain insights from those who have walked the path before you. In this chapter, we'll explore the importance of networking and mentorship, how to find the right connections, and how these relationships can support your business's growth.

**The Importance of Networking**

1. **Expanding Your Connections:**

- **Business Opportunities:** Networking helps you connect with other business owners, industry professionals, and potential clients, opening doors to new opportunities and partnerships.
    - **Resource Sharing:** Through networking, you can access resources, information, and advice that can help you manage your business credit, secure financing, and grow your business.
2. **Building Credibility:**
    - **Reputation Building:** Being active in your business community enhances your reputation and credibility. A strong network can lead to referrals, recommendations, and increased trust in your business.
    - **Peer Support:** Networking with other business owners provides a support system where you can share experiences, challenges, and solutions.
3. **Learning and Growth:**
    - **Industry Insights:** Networking keeps you informed about industry trends, market changes, and new opportunities that can impact your business.
    - **Skill Development:** Engaging with other professionals allows you to learn new skills, gain fresh perspectives, and improve your business practices.

**The Role of Mentorship**

1. **Guidance and Support:**
    - **Expert Advice:** A mentor provides valuable advice based on their own experiences, helping you navigate challenges, avoid common pitfalls, and make informed decisions.

- **Personalized Feedback:** Mentors offer personalized feedback on your business strategies, credit management, and financial decisions, helping you refine your approach.

2. **Accountability:**
   - **Goal Setting:** A mentor helps you set realistic goals and holds you accountable for achieving them. This accountability can motivate you to stay focused and disciplined.
   - **Long-Term Vision:** Mentorship encourages you to think long-term about your business's growth and success, helping you develop a strategic vision and plan.

3. **Confidence Building:**
   - **Encouragement:** Mentors provide encouragement and reassurance, helping you build confidence in your abilities and decisions.
   - **Risk Management:** With a mentor's guidance, you can approach risks with greater confidence, knowing that you have a trusted advisor to turn to.

**How to Find Networking Opportunities**

1. **Join Industry Associations:**
   - **Membership Benefits:** Industry associations often provide networking events, conferences, and online forums where you can connect with other professionals in your field.
   - **Professional Development:** Many associations offer workshops, webinars, and training sessions that can enhance your skills and knowledge.

2. **Attend Business Events:**

- **Local Meetups:** Look for local business meetups, networking events, and trade shows in your area. These events provide opportunities to connect with other business owners and industry leaders.
- **Chamber of Commerce:** Joining your local Chamber of Commerce can provide access to networking events, business resources, and community involvement opportunities.

3. **Utilize Online Platforms:**
   - **LinkedIn:** Use LinkedIn to connect with other professionals, join industry groups, and participate in discussions related to your field.
   - **Networking Apps:** Apps like Meetup, Eventbrite, and Shapr offer opportunities to find and join networking events in your area or online.

4. **Participate in Webinars and Virtual Events:**
   - **Online Conferences:** Many organizations host virtual conferences and webinars that provide networking opportunities, even if you can't attend in person.
   - **Interactive Sessions:** Look for webinars that include Q&A sessions, breakout rooms, or networking opportunities to connect with other attendees.

## How to Find a Mentor

1. **Leverage Existing Networks:**
   - **Professional Connections:** Start by reaching out to your existing professional network, including colleagues, former

bosses, and industry contacts, to see if they can recommend a mentor.
    - **Industry Associations:** Many industry associations offer mentorship programs that pair experienced professionals with newer business owners.
2. **Use Mentorship Platforms:**
    - **Score:** SCORE is a nonprofit organization that provides free mentoring to small business owners. You can connect with experienced business mentors through their online platform.
    - **MicroMentor:** An online platform that connects entrepreneurs with volunteer business mentors from around the world.
3. **Join Business Incubators or Accelerators:**
    - **Incubators:** Business incubators often provide mentorship as part of their support services, helping startups and small businesses grow and succeed.
    - **Accelerators:** Accelerators typically offer intensive mentorship and support for businesses looking to scale quickly. These programs often include access to experienced mentors and industry experts.
4. **Seek Out Peer Mentorship:**
    - **Peer Groups:** Join peer mentorship groups or mastermind groups where business owners at similar stages of growth can share experiences, challenges, and advice.
    - **Reciprocal Mentorship:** Consider offering your own skills and experience in exchange for mentorship from someone in a complementary field.

**Free and Low-Cost Resources**

Here are some resources to help you find networking opportunities and mentorship:

- **SCORE:** A free resource that provides mentoring, workshops, and business advice to small business owners.
- **MicroMentor:** An online platform that connects entrepreneurs with volunteer business mentors.
- **LinkedIn Groups:** Join industry-specific LinkedIn groups to connect with professionals, participate in discussions, and find potential mentors.

**Encouragement: Building Relationships for Success**

Networking and mentorship are about more than just making connections—they're about building relationships that support your business's growth and success. By surrounding yourself with knowledgeable, experienced, and supportive individuals, you're creating a network of resources that you can rely on as you navigate the challenges of building and growing your business credit. Remember, you don't have to do it alone. Reach out, connect, and let these relationships help guide you toward your goals.

## Chapter 16: Staying Up-to-Date with Business Credit Trends

The world of business credit is constantly evolving, with new trends, tools, and regulations emerging regularly. Staying informed about these changes is crucial for maintaining and growing your business credit. In this chapter, we'll discuss how to stay up-to-date with the latest business credit trends, the importance of continuous learning, and where to find reliable information.

**Why Staying Informed is Important**

1. **Adapting to Changes:**
   - **Regulatory Updates:** Changes in business credit regulations, such as updates to credit reporting practices or new lending laws, can impact your business. Staying informed helps you adapt and ensure compliance.
   - **New Opportunities:** Emerging trends, such as new credit-building tools or alternative financing options, can provide opportunities to improve your credit profile or access funding.
2. **Maintaining Competitive Advantage:**
   - **Industry Insights:** Keeping up with industry trends and best practices allows you to stay ahead of competitors and make informed decisions that enhance your business's financial health.
   - **Innovation:** By staying informed, you can take advantage of innovative tools, strategies, and technologies that can help you build and manage your business credit more effectively.
3. **Risk Management:**
   - **Identifying Risks:** Awareness of potential risks, such as economic downturns or changes in credit markets, allows you to take proactive steps to protect your business.

- **Preparedness:** Being informed helps you prepare for challenges, whether they're related to credit access, financial management, or market conditions.

**How to Stay Informed**

1. **Follow Industry Blogs and News Sites:**
   - **Credit Monitoring Services:** Many credit monitoring services, like Nav and Credit Karma, offer blogs and articles on business credit trends, providing insights and updates on the latest developments.
   - **Business News Sites:** Websites like Bloomberg, Forbes, and The Wall Street Journal regularly cover topics related to business credit, lending, and finance.
2. **Subscribe to Newsletters:**
   - **Industry Newsletters:** Subscribe to newsletters from credit bureaus, financial institutions, and business organizations to receive updates on credit trends, regulatory changes, and new credit products.
   - **Credit Education Platforms:** Platforms like Experian and Dun & Bradstreet offer newsletters that provide tips, news, and resources related to business credit.
3. **Attend Webinars and Conferences:**
   - **Online Webinars:** Many organizations offer free or low-cost webinars on business credit, financing, and financial management. These events often feature experts who provide the latest insights and strategies.

- **Industry Conferences:** Attend industry conferences, either in person or virtually, to learn about emerging trends, network with other professionals, and gain new knowledge.

4. **Join Professional Organizations:**
   - **Membership Benefits:** Professional organizations, such as the National Association of Credit Management (NACM), offer resources, training, and networking opportunities that keep you informed about industry trends.
   - **Certifications:** Consider pursuing certifications in credit management or business finance, which often include access to exclusive resources and continuing education.

5. **Engage in Online Communities:**
   - **Discussion Forums:** Join online forums and communities, such as those on Reddit, LinkedIn, or industry-specific platforms, where business owners and professionals share insights, experiences, and advice.
   - **Social Media Groups:** Follow relevant social media groups and pages on platforms like Facebook and Twitter to stay updated on business credit news and trends.

**Free and Low-Cost Resources**

Here are some resources to help you stay up-to-date with business credit trends:

- **Nav Blog:** Offers articles and updates on business credit, financing, and financial management.

- **Experian Business Resources:** Provides educational content, webinars, and newsletters on business credit and financial health.
- **National Association of Credit Management (NACM):** Offers resources, training, and networking opportunities for credit professionals.

**Encouragement: Embracing Continuous Learning**

The world of business credit is dynamic and ever-changing, and staying informed is key to maintaining your business's financial health. By embracing continuous learning and staying updated on the latest trends and developments, you're positioning your business for long-term success. Remember, knowledge is power—especially when it comes to managing your business credit. Stay curious, stay informed, and use what you learn to make informed decisions that drive your business forward.

## Chapter 17: Purchasing Property Under Your LLC

Purchasing property under your LLC (Limited Liability Company) is a strategic way to generate monthly income while protecting your personal assets. This chapter will guide you through the exact steps to take and provide you with the necessary resources to successfully buy and manage a property under your LLC.

**Step 1: Form Your LLC**

**Choose Your LLC Name:**

- **Unique and Compliant:** Ensure the name is unique and complies with your state's LLC naming rules.
- **Availability Check:** Check your state's business registry to ensure the name is available.

**File Articles of Organization:**

- **Submit to State:** Submit this document to your state's business filing office, typically the Secretary of State.
- **Fee Payment:** Pay the required filing fee.

**Create an Operating Agreement:**

- **Management Structure:** Outline the management structure and operating procedures of your LLC.
- **Internal Document:** While not always required by law, this document is important for internal governance.

**Obtain an EIN:**

- **Tax Identification:** Apply for an Employer Identification Number (EIN) from the IRS for tax purposes.
- **Free Application:** The application is free and can be done online.

**Register for State Taxes:**

- **State Requirements:** Depending on your state, you might need to register for state taxes or obtain specific permits.

**Step 2: Set Up a Business Bank Account**

**Open a Business Checking Account:**

- **EIN Required:** Use your LLC's EIN to open the account.
- **Separate Finances:** Keep your business and personal finances separate to protect your LLC's liability status.

**Keep Finances Separate:**

- **All Transactions:** Ensure all income and expenses related to the property are handled through this account.

### Step 3: Secure Financing

**Build Business Credit:**

- **Vendor Accounts:** Establish credit by opening lines of credit in the LLC's name.
- **Credit Monitoring:** Regularly monitor your business credit.

**Research Loan Options:**

- **Commercial Loans:** Look for lenders that offer commercial real estate loans for LLCs.
- **Compare Terms:** Compare interest rates, loan terms, and fees from different lenders.

**Get Pre-Approved:**

- **Pre-Approval Letter:** Obtain a pre-approval letter from your lender, which shows sellers that you're a serious buyer.

### Step 4: Search for Income-Generating Properties

**Determine Your Budget:**

- **Financing Impact:** Based on your financing, set your budget.
- **Cash Flow Considerations:** Consider the potential rental income versus the costs of the property.

**Select the Type of Property:**

- **Residential or Commercial:** Decide between residential or commercial properties based on your investment goals.
- **Market Research:** Research the local market to find areas with strong rental demand.

**Work with a Real Estate Agent:**

- **Investment Experience:** Find an agent experienced in investment properties.
- **Property Search:** Have your agent identify properties that meet your criteria.

**Evaluate Properties:**

- **Due Diligence:** Consider location, potential rental income, property condition, and necessary renovations.

**Step 5: Make an Offer**

**Submit an Offer Through Your LLC:**

- **LLC Name:** Ensure the offer is made in the name of your LLC.
- **Legal Review:** Have your attorney review the offer before submission.

**Negotiate Terms:**

- **Purchase Price:** Work with your agent to negotiate the purchase price and contingencies.

**Sign a Purchase Agreement:**

- **Legal Binding:** Sign a legally binding purchase agreement outlining the sale terms.

### Step 6: Conduct Due Diligence

**Property Inspection:**

- **Professional Inspector:** Hire a professional inspector to assess the property's condition.

**Appraisal:**

- **Lender Requirement:** Your lender will require an appraisal to ensure the property's value matches the loan amount.

**Title Search and Insurance:**

- **Clear Title:** Conduct a title search and purchase title insurance to protect against future claims.

### Step 7: Close the Deal

**Finalize Financing:**

- **Loan Finalization:** Work with your lender to finalize the loan.

**Review Closing Documents:**

- **Careful Review:** Review all documents, including the deed, loan agreement, and settlement statement.

**Close on the Property:**

- **Closing Meeting:** Attend the closing meeting to sign all necessary documents.

**Step 8: Set Up Property Management**

**Decide on Management:**

- **Self-Management or Company:** Choose whether to manage the property yourself or hire a property management company.

**Prepare the Property for Rent:**

- **Necessary Repairs:** Make necessary repairs or renovations.
- **Market the Property:** Determine competitive rent and advertise the property.

**Step 9: Screen Tenants**

**Tenant Application Process:**

- **Rental Application:** Require potential tenants to complete a rental application.

**Run Background and Credit Checks:**

- **Tenant Verification:** Verify the tenant's background and credit history.

**Sign Lease Agreements:**

- **LLC Name:** Draft a lease agreement in the name of your LLC.

### Step 10: Manage the Property and Finances

**Collect Rent:**

- **Direct Payments:** Ensure rent payments are made directly to your LLC's bank account.

**Maintain the Property:**

- **Regular Maintenance:** Regularly maintain the property to keep it in good condition.

**Record Keeping:**

- **Detailed Records:** Keep detailed records of all income, expenses, and maintenance activities.

### Step 11: Maximize Income and Plan for Expansion

**Increase Rent Strategically:**

- **Rent Increases:** Consider increasing rent when leases are renewed.

**Reduce Expenses:**

- **Cost Management:** Look for ways to reduce expenses without compromising the property's value.

**Plan for Additional Investments:**

- **Expansion:** Use cash flow or equity to invest in additional properties.

**Additional Resources for Property Investment**

- **Roofstock:** A marketplace for buying and selling rental properties.
- **BiggerPockets:** A community and resource hub for real estate investors.
- **RealtyMogul:** For investing in commercial real estate.

**Encouragement: Building Wealth Through Real Estate**

By following these steps, you can successfully purchase a property under your LLC, generate monthly income, and build a profitable real estate investment portfolio. With the right planning and management, your property can become a valuable asset that contributes to your long-term financial success.

---

## Conclusion: Empowering Your Business Journey

Building and managing business credit is more than just a financial exercise—it's a critical component of your business's growth, stability, and success. By following the strategies outlined in this book, from establishing vendor credit to leveraging advanced financing options, you're taking control of your business's financial future.

Remember, building business credit is a journey that requires discipline, persistence, and continuous learning. Whether you're just starting out or looking to take your business to the next level, the tools, tips, and resources provided in this book are designed to empower you every step of the way.

As you continue on your journey, keep in mind the importance of staying informed, building strong relationships, and making informed decisions. Your business credit is a powerful tool—use it wisely, and it will open doors to new opportunities, growth, and long-term success.

Thank you for taking the time to invest in your business's future by reading this book. I wish you the best of luck on your journey to building a strong and thriving business.

## Appendix: Additional Resources

### 1. Business Credit Monitoring:

- **Nav.com:** Offers free and paid business credit monitoring tools.
- **Credit Karma:** Provides free credit monitoring, including alerts for changes in your credit report.

### 2. Business Planning:

- **SBA Business Plan Tool:** A free guide to creating a comprehensive business plan.
- **LivePlan:** Paid business planning software with tools for creating financial projections.

### 3. Networking and Mentorship:

- **SCORE:** Free mentoring and workshops for small business owners.
- **LinkedIn:** A professional networking platform for connecting with industry peers.

4. **Real Estate Investment:**

- **Roofstock:** A platform for buying and selling rental properties.
- **BiggerPockets:** A community for real estate investors to share knowledge and resources.

5. **Free Resources for Credit Building:**

- **SBA Microloan Program:** Small loans for startups and small businesses.
- **Kiva:** Interest-free microloans for small businesses and entrepreneurs.

6. **Legal and Tax Resources:**

- **IRS EIN Application:** Apply for an Employer Identification Number online.
- **Nolo:** Provides legal guides and forms for small business owners.

## Copyright Information

**Title:** Building Business Credit from Scratch: A Simple Guide for Entrepreneurs
**Author:** Felisha Weaver
**Publisher:**

**ISBN:**
**Date of Publication:** 08/10/24

**Copyright:** ©2024 Felisha Weaver. All rights reserved. No part of this book may be reproduced or transmitted in any form or by any means, electronic or mechanical, including photocopying, recording, or by any information storage and retrieval system, without permission in writing from the publisher.

www.ingramcontent.com/pod-product-compliance
Lightning Source LLC
Chambersburg PA
CBHW071936210526
45479CB00002B/709